Bismarck: 24 Hours to Doom

Iain Ballantyne is the award-winning author of military and naval history books, and contributor to television news and documentary programmes, and radio shows. In 2021 his *Bismarck: 24 Hours to Doom* was the subject of a major television documentary broadcast in the UK by Channel 4. Iain is a former newspaper reporter and currently Editor of a globally read defence magazine, occasionally writing for other publications. His other books include *The Deadly Trade* (Weidenfeld & Nicolson), a history of submarine warfare and *Hunter Killers* (Orion), covering the Cold War undersea confrontation. He is the host of Warships Pod.

Follow him on Twitter @IBallantyn

Also by Iain Ballantyne

Arnhem: Ten Days in the Cauldron
Bismarck: 24 Hours to Doom

IAIN BALLANTYNE

BISMARCK

24 HOURS TO DOOM

CANELOHISTORY

First published in the United Kingdom in 2016 by Ipso Books

This edition published in the United Kingdom in 2023 by

Canelo
Unit 9, 5th Floor
Cargo Works, 1–2 Hatfields
London SE1 9PG
United Kingdom

A CIP catalogue record for this book is available from the British Library.

Print ISBN 978 1 80436 340 9
Ebook ISBN 978 1 80436 341 6

The *Bismarck* Action map by Dennis Andrews, revised by Steve Jagger
Pursuit and Crippling of *Bismarck* map by Steve Jagger
The Final Battle map by Dennis Andrews, revised by Steve Jagger

Cover design by Philip Beresford

Look for more great books at www.canelo.co

Printed and bound in Great Britain by Clays Ltd, Elcograf S.p.A.

1

MIX
Paper from
responsible sources
FSC® C018072
www.fsc.org

Dedicated to the veterans of the Bismarck Action

23–27 May 1941

'What a life it is, this War!?'

—Royal Marine Len Nicholl, HMS *Rodney*

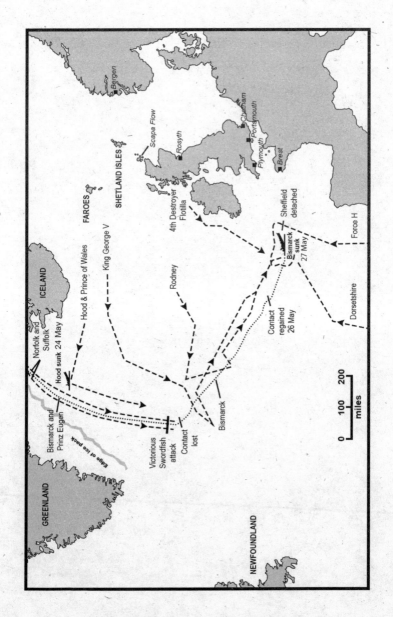

The *Bismarck* Action: 23–27 May 1941

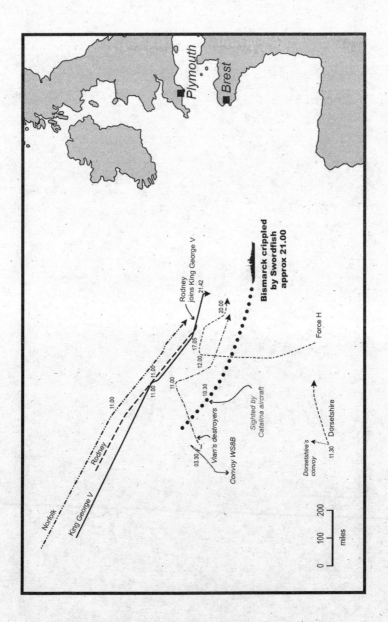

Pursuit and Crippling of *Bismarck*: 26 May 1941

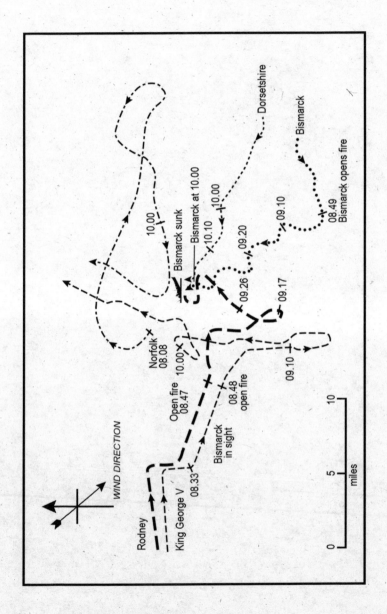

The Final Battle: 27 May 1941

Foreword

Rear Admiral Martin Connell, CBE,
Head of the Fleet Air Arm

The epic hunt for the *Bismarck* evokes many memories from my own time as a junior Royal Navy officer. My first ship was the Type 22 frigate HMS *Sheffield*, named after both the destroyer of the same name lost in the Falklands in 1982, and before that the Town Class cruiser which took part in the hunt for the *Bismarck* in 1941.

We would on occasion watch the Lewis Gilbert film *Sink the Bismarck*, and, as a young Fleet Air Arm officer, I can clearly recall the gentle barracking I received from my fellow officers when the film gets to the part where the Swordfish aircraft mistakenly attack HMS *Sheffield* thinking it is the *Bismarck*. How could this possibly happen? I now realise that such incidents can easily occur amidst the confusion of naval operations, particularly when the weather is marginal, communications are restricted, and the surface warfare picture is confused. It was an important early lesson for me.

I had the privilege of hosting Iain Ballantyne onboard HMS *Chatham* when I was in command in the northern Gulf in 2008. While he was of course interested in our mission and the geopolitics of the region, what struck me most was his interest in the human stories of each of my sailors. We were a Devonport ship and there were many West Country natives onboard, and Iain was keen to hear their perspectives, what made them tick, what they missed most from home.

Naval warfare is, after all, fundamentally a human endeavour, only enabled by technology, where one commander is seeking to outwit their adversary, and it is often played out across a vast seascape extending thousands of miles and nearly always out of sight, where the outcome can have strategic implications. Perhaps this is why the enormity of the loss of life from the sinking of HMS *Hood* in May 1941 shook the government at the time to its very core. The loss of life of over 1,400 sailors whose bodies would forever remain in a watery grave came as a huge shock to the nation and brought home the cost of naval warfare. It also placed a particular responsibility and burden on those fortunate enough to survive to ensure their deceased shipmates' voices and experiences were heard.

The humanity which underpins the *Bismarck* story is brilliantly captured in this book, which serves as an oral history to the dramatic events as they unfolded in those final decisive hours. The quotes meticulously drawn from veterans and survivors on both sides enables us all to imagine being immersed in the action as the epic chase unfolds, whether it be on the bridge of the warships, in the cockpit of the Swordfish biplanes, or in the cold, damp claustrophobic messdecks where sailors anxiously awaited their next call to action.

Much of the drama of the pursuit of *Bismarck* takes place in the unforgiving North Atlantic. Having spent many weeks in various classes of warships patrolling the Atlantic, I know only too well how unforgiving it can be, particularly when you are hunting for submarines or operating aircraft from small, moving flight decks exposed to the elements. The ocean's strategic importance in terms of access and the free movement of trade endures to the present day.

It is therefore perhaps fitting that exactly 80 years on from those epic few days in May 1941, another Royal Navy task group of ships will deploy out into those very same Atlantic waters. The aircraft carrier HMS *Queen Elizabeth* and her task group of frigates, destroyers, aircraft, and support ships will venture out on their inaugural operational deployment, and 4,000 sailors, airmen, and marines will begin to write the next chapter of Atlantic naval operations.

As Rear Admiral Fleet Air Arm and the Royal Navy's Director Force Generation, I know all too well just how much work goes in to preparing for such a deployment. But I also know that once deployed, it must ultimately be left to the men and women onboard those ships to determine the numerous day-to-day tactical decisions which occur, and the human stories, fears, and motivations which underpin each and every one of them.

Introduction

Specially published to mark the 80th anniversary of the *Bismarck* Action, this new edition of *Bismarck: 24 Hours to Doom* includes additional perspectives on the epic events of late May 1941 not to be found in the earlier version, or my previous books on the episode.

Bismarck: 24 Hours to Doom (Agora Books) is part of what I like to call my '*Bismarck* trilogy', the other two works being *HMS Rodney* (2008) and *Killing the Bismarck* (2010), both published by Pen & Sword.

Each book offers different perspectives on the famous *Bismarck* Action. With the human experience at the fore, and presenting, in each case, distinct variations of style and substantial amounts of unique content, the trilogy offers: a broad-ranging look at the entire Action, from the events prior to the *Hood*'s destruction through to the *Bismarck*'s sinking and the aftermath (*Killing the Bismarck*); the life story of the battleship that did the most to sink the *Bismarck* and saw much other service in the Second World War (*HMS Rodney*); and, in this book, a cinematic telling of the final 24 hours of the episode, which aims to be fast-paced, action-packed, and concise.

At this the new edition's heart remain unique accounts by combat veterans, using transcripts of my filmed interviews with participants of the *Bismarck* Action. I remain in their debt for often speaking with raw honesty about the reality of sea warfare in the age of battleships, a vanished era which lived on so vividly in their minds.

Now that the veterans who were there have passed away, it is even more of a special privilege to be the conduit for their experiences. To have spoken at length to them – teasing out the detail of what they experienced, conveying their feelings about one of the most epic and brutal engagements in naval history – enables me to present this powerful story, much of it in their own words. In that way, they put us in a ringside seat for history in the making.

—Iain Ballantyne, May 2021.

–

For more about Iain Ballantyne's books on the *Bismarck* Action, visit bismarckbattle.com

Prologue

A pall of gloom and anxiety is draped over Britain. It is reeling in shock from the loss of the biggest and most beautiful warship in the Royal Navy (RN) – the 48,360-ton battlecruiser HMS *Hood*.

For two decades she has been an icon of the British Empire, but on 24 May 1941, *The Mighty Hood* was blown apart after a mere eight minutes of combat with the new Nazi battleship *Bismarck* in the Denmark Strait.

An attempt by the 50,000-ton steel monster, to break out into the Atlantic and ravage vital convoys to the United Kingdom – aiming to sink merchant vessels carrying armaments, oil, iron ore, timber and food among other things crucial to maintaining the war effort – has been expected by the British for months. On 20 May, that great fear about a *Bismarck* sortie becomes reality.

Spotted from the shores of Scandinavia by British spies as she exits the Baltic, the *Bismarck* is in company with the heavy cruiser *Prinz Eugen*, which, like the battleship, will endeavour to roam the Atlantic creating chaos and inflicting destruction in the shipping lanes.

Extraordinarily, the supreme commander of the German armed forces, Adolf Hitler has been kept in the dark by the German naval top brass about plans for the foray. Hitler was only told about it once the ships had deployed.

The leaders of the Kriegsmarine feared the Führer would ban it altogether, due to anxiety about losing the national flagship, having already suffered heavy losses in surface ships at the hands of the Royal Navy. Most notably, Germany suffered the loss of commerce raider *Admiral Graf Spee*, which was hunted to destruction by RN cruisers in the South Atlantic during December 1939.

–

In May 1941 as *Bismarck* headed north, close to the shores of Nazi-occupied Norway, sailors sang as they happily went about their chores on the upper deck of the battleship.

When the *Bismarck* and *Prinz Eugen* called at the Grimstadfjord, south of Bergen, to take on supplies, their sailors admired the vista. *Bismarck*'s 20-year-old junior rating Rudolf Römer asked an officer to loan him binoculars so he could study 'the brightly-coloured houses on the hillside' which he found 'really pretty'. Young officer Hans Georg Stiegler, aged 21, gazed at Norwegians having breakfast picnics on the shore and thought it 'such a peaceful scene.' Otto Peters, a 22-year-old stoker, was less at ease and felt those pretty houses and picnic groups must contain spies reporting back on the presence of the two German ships to the British.

In fact, he was right. Having been tipped off by Norwegians about the presence of the German battleships, the British forces had already sent a Royal Air Force (RAF) Spitfire reconnaissance aircraft to confirm *Bismarck* and *Prinz Eugen* were in the Grimstadfjord.

At 1.15 pm on 21 May, alarm klaxons sounded out in the ships, disturbing the idyll. Otto Peters happened to be working on the upper deck and scanned the sky, spotting a tiny British aircraft as 'it shot out from among the clouds and then vanished again'.

Despite the RAF discovering them, that evening the two ships headed out into the North Atlantic and began their transit around the north of Iceland.

Sighted shortly after 7.00 pm on 23 May, and shadowed by the British heavy cruisers *Suffolk* and *Norfolk*, the German battleship and her raiding partner made a high-speed run through the narrow waters between Greenland and Iceland.

The *Hood*, sent north from the main Home Fleet anchorage at Scapa Flow in the Orkney Islands to intercept the Germans, suffered gravely. Only three men out of the ship's company of 1,418 survived the Denmark Strait clash, and the brand-new battleship *Prince of Wales* withdrew badly damaged.

After the loss of the *Hood*, the London correspondent of the *New York Times*, Robert P Post, writes in a 'special cable' to American readers:

> *The news of the Hood's sinking is bound to cast a spell of gloom over the British people, because she was a symbol of British naval power.*

In pubs, homes, and on street corners – wherever people gather – the terrible news is discussed. The shock is real and painful, for with the Army beaten and ejected from Europe and the RAF victory over the Luftwaffe in the summer of 1940 providing only a brief respite, a vital struggle for survival is unfolding in the Atlantic.

The surface raiders and U-boats of the Kriegsmarine are trying to force Britain into a peace deal that will let Germany focus all its military power on invading and conquering the Soviet Union.

The Royal Navy, which for centuries has ruled the waves appears to be losing the war of the oceans. It is stretched too thin across the seven seas.

Nowhere is the news of the *Hood*'s loss more keenly felt than in the British warships, where the men aboard learned of the catastrophe within minutes via a global wireless signals net. RN ships rarely send such signals, to avoid giving their positions away to the enemy, but they can read those made both by the Admiralty and other British naval vessels without exposing themselves. In this way they get a minute-by-minute insight into what is happening.

Thus, early on the morning of 24 May, warships decrypt a shocking signal from the *Norfolk*, which, along with the *Suffolk*, witnessed the cataclysmic event. *Norfolk* tells the Admiralty in London:

> *HOOD blown up...*

Rear Admiral Frederic Wake-Walker aboard *Norfolk* instructs nearby destroyers:

> *Proceed and search for survivors.*

–

At that moment, the *Hood* survivors are each clinging to small rafts, or 'biscuit floats', tossed around on the cold North Atlantic swell.

Junior rating Ted Briggs is aged just 18 and a signaller who had joined the *Hood* in July 1939, fulfilling a boyhood dream of serving in the legendary warship. As the *Hood* sank – the heart of the ship ripped out by a series of massive explosions – Briggs managed to escape from the bridge of the battle-cruiser, but then…

> *'I felt myself being dragged down, but you get to the stage [where] you just can't hold your breath anymore. What it put me in mind of later was a Tom and Jerry cartoon where Tom the cat was in the river and he was drowning – he was going under – and I felt like that. It was quiet resignation, actually. I suddenly seemed to shoot to the surface … and I looked around and there was Hood, vertical in the water, about fifty yards away, and B turret was just going under. I panicked, and I turned and swam as fast as I could away from her. When I looked around again, she'd gone, but there was a fire on the water where she'd been. The water was about four inches thick with oil, and again I panicked. I turned again and swam. When I looked around the second time, the fire had gone out and over, on the other side, I could see these two other people … there wasn't another soul in sight.'*

Midshipman Bill Dundas, aged 18, who had also been on the bridge of the battlecruiser, escaped by climbing through a window. The other survivor is 20-year-old junior rating Robert Tilburn, at the time of the battle assigned to the crew of a 4-inch gun on the exposed Boat Deck of the *Hood*.

While many of his shipmates were slaughtered as enemy shells screamed in, Tilburn was saved by an urge to throw up. Having just seen a fellow gunner, who was also taking cover on the deck, disembowelled by shrapnel, Tilburn was also caught in a shower of body parts – the remains of sailors and Royal Marines blown apart as the cataclysmic series of explosions ripped *Hood* asunder.

Vomiting over the side of the ship, Tilburn noticed that the vessel appeared to be rapidly sinking by the stern. Spotting a large piece of debris hurtling in his direction, Tilburn leapt out of the way.

Deciding it was time to abandon ship, in the midst of divesting himself of duffel coat, helmet and gas mask – accoutrements of war that would weigh him down – a rising sea swept Tilburn away.

Then, as the ship rolled over, a mast smacked down next to him, with one of Tilburn's boot-shod feet snared by a radio aerial. He was tugged under as some of *Hood*'s shattered remains sank, but Tilburn somehow retrieved a knife that he carried.

'I managed to cut my seaboot off and free myself, and when I came to the top [surface] just the bows were stuck out of the water, practically vertical, and then she slid under.'

–

Bobbing on an empty ocean, prospects of being saved seem slim, but the three young men keep their rafts close together with desperate hope in their hearts, though the icy weather is getting to Briggs. 'We managed to get together and started to hold onto each other and oh, it was so cold, we just couldn't hold on, and gradually we started to drift apart.'

The cold sleep of death begins to creep over Tilburn and Briggs, but Dundas urges them to stay awake and starts singing songs, telling them to join in: 'Roll out the barrel, let's have a barrel of fun...'

An RAF Sunderland flying boat passes over but fails to spot them. Still trying to keep them all awake, Dundas suggests they tell each other the stories of how they survived *Hood*'s sinking. But this tires them out, so they stop talking.

Dundas again roars 'Roll Out the Barrel', but the other two do not join in. Briggs feels a 'sleepy mist' invading his brain.

Salvation for the *Hood*'s survivors arrives four hours after the ship went down, in the shape of the destroyer HMS *Electra*.

She comes over the horizon from the North at high speed, sailors on her upper decks scanning the surface of the sea for signs of life.

–

Jack Taylor is a junior rating in *Electra* and earlier listened to the rumbling of the guns and explosions in the far distance as battle in the Denmark Strait began and quickly ceased.

As she sped to the scene of the battle, a broadcast was made to the destroyer's crew, telling them 'to make ready to pick up survivors' with Taylor and his shipmates anticipating their vessel would soon be crowded.

> *'We made ready to pick up hundreds of injured and wounded men from the grey cold sea. We could not turn out our boats as they were smashed [by earlier stormy weather], hanging in the davits. Blankets, medical supplies, hot beverages, and rum were got ready. Scrambling nets were flung over the ship's side, trailing into the water. Men were lining the side ready with hand lines, eyes straining into the greyness*

9

ahead. It was only what seemed like a matter of minutes when we broke out of a mist patch into the clear. And there it was. The place where the Hood had sunk. Wreckage of all descriptions was floating on the surface. Hammocks, broken rafts, boots, clothes, caps. Of the hundreds of men we expected to see there was no sign. An awestruck moment and a shipmate next to me exclaimed: "Good Lord, she's gone with all hands!" We nosed our way slowly amongst all the pitiful remains of books, letters, photos, and other personal effects floating by...'

–

On his float, Ted Briggs hears one of the others cry out.

It is Bill Dundas 'who had managed to sit up on his raft and was looking round saying, "There's a ship over there" and I looked. I could see "H27" [on the ship's hull] which was *Electra*, I was calling out: "Electra! Electra!" And the other two joined in with me.'

As the *Electra* reaches them, a senior rating aboard the destroyer throws a rope to Briggs, which he grabs.

The senior rating yells:

'Don't you let go of that!'

Briggs shouts back:

'*You bet your bloody life I won't!*'

Jack Taylor goes down a scrambling net hung over the side of the *Electra* with other sailors until 'the water was around our knees'...

> '*We hung onto the net, our arms outstretched as the first man floated alongside. Quickly we grabbed him and lifted him onto the net. Careful hands on deck reached down and hauled him up to the deck.*'

After being helped aboard the *Electra*, the priority – under the supervision of the destroyer's doctor and sick berth attendants – is to warm the survivors up, removing their oil-soaked clothing.

Briggs finds himself and the others soon wrapped in blankets and remembers, 'they filled us full of rum, which was a good thing really, because we'd swallowed some oil and it made us violently ill'. And so, in this fashion, the survivors bring it up.

A search is mounted for other survivors, but none are found. When Taylor and his shipmates in the *Electra* again scan the surrounding seascape, searching 'for a long time among what remained of this once proud ship', there is nothing more to be found.

'With a heavy heart we turned away as we could do no more.'

As the *Bismarck* heads south in company with the *Prinz Eugen*, the German sailors celebrate the terrific victory they have just achieved over a navy that has become accustomed to ruling the waves.

The men in one of *Bismarck*'s 15-inch gun turrets play a dance tune on a record player while there are champagne toasts to the enemy's defeat in the wardroom. In the engine room of the *Bismarck*, Otto Peters finds that, on being informed 'the *Hood* has blown up ... to tell truth we were happy, but not overwhelmingly happy, which is understandable...' He feels that had the *Hood* destroyed the *Bismarck* then 'on the other side it would have been the same'.

The *Bismarck* has lost no men but did not come through her first battle unscathed. The Prinz *Eugen* may have got away without being hit by the British, but *Prince of Wales* scored three 14-inch shell hits on the German flagship. One punched through her bows, causing flooding and puncturing a fuel tank. With 2,000 tons of sea water gushing in, the ship is down by the bows and losing oil, though the holes are plugged. Another shell hit the *Bismarck* amidships below the water line, flooding the port generator room and other spaces, with Port Boiler Room 2 suffering partial flooding. The third 14-inch shell smashed through a wooden boat, with fragments damaging the catapult for launching the ship's aircraft. Apparently superficial, these hits will come to have a great effect on the German vessel's fate.

–

The young men of the British fleet are veterans of combat from the moment hostilities began in September 1939. There never was a phoney war at sea but the loss of the *Hood* – a beloved relic of the First World War that should have been replaced years before – is still a terrible blow.

Now they reflect on the sudden destruction of a ship many have served in and also the deaths of men and boys whom many of them knew.

Above all, they realise the job of hunting down the *Bismarck* now falls to other ships currently scattered far and wide across the Atlantic. All it needs is for the net to be drawn tight, but *Bismarck* could, nonetheless, still escape and sew chaos on the high seas.

The disruption caused by German surface raiders is a serious threat to national survival. With just one or two high-speed, well-armed enemy battleships (or cruisers) on the loose, the complex system that feeds the war effort may falter, at a time when only Britain is still in the fight against the Nazis.

Fear alone causes hundreds, if not thousands, of cancelled sailings, delays deliveries, and forces the Admiralty to take warships away from directly fighting the enemy to protect otherwise defenceless vessels.

An industrial powerhouse, with a population of 48 million, island nation Britain depends on its large Merchant Navy and also the cargo ships of neutral nations. It needs them to deliver 50 percent of its food, 100 percent of its oil, and most of the raw materials for industry.

Without oil, warplanes cannot fly, warships are unable to leave port, and armoured vehicles are rendered immobile. Should the supply of raw material diminish too much, the wheels of war production will grind to a halt. Civilians might find their rations reduced.

Rather than seeking to avoid starvation, it is a case of ensuring merchant ships carry cargos such as iron ore, munitions, and finished weapons to Britain, in order to maintain the fight, rather than packing ship holds with bananas and oranges. Keeping war industries going relies on preventing the enemy from ravaging crucial convoys, above all from Canada and the USA, but also protecting trade from South America and Australia.

In September 1939, Britain was importing close to 77 million tons of goods and raw materials per annum, yet by 1941 this has been more than halved. The British also need to maintain exports to keep their economy afloat, but these have dwindled dangerously with all that industry can produce needed at home.

Post-war, German submarines will be seen as the most dangerous threat to Britain's transatlantic lifelines, but, in 1941, the surface raiders are equally feared, especially *Bismarck* as the biggest, most modern, and best armed.

Between late 1940 to spring 1941, less powerful German surface raiders had already taken a heavy toll of British sea trade. Between January and March 1941, two of them – the battlecruisers *Scharnhorst* and *Gneisenau* – sank 115,000 tons of shipping, representing 22 valuable merchant vessels lost to the British cause; several were also captured.

That the toll was not higher could be attributed to the use of Royal Navy battleships on convoy escort work. German surface raiders are usually ordered to avoid confrontation with enemy capital ships, according to their naval high command's instructions, and even the *Bismarck* is meant to do the same when there appears to be 'excessive risk'. But the *Bismarck* found the confrontation with the *Hood* and *Prince of Wales* unavoidable, and now – as a proven capital ship killer – she may well claim another warship scalp or two in addition to sinking merchant vessels.

Another dimension of the threat she poses is psychological and strategic. That Britannia rules the waves underpins her security as well as the ability to feed her people and factories. Should the Royal Navy prove unable to maintain that supremacy – should it be shattered by the *Bismarck* laying waste to merchant shipping and getting away with blowing apart Royal Navy capital ships – the will of the British people to carry on fighting may collapse. Suppliers of critical war materials and food, primarily America and Canada, may see Britain as a bankrupt, spent power that it is not worth backing.

Winston Churchill, in his twin capacity as Britain's Prime Minister (PM) and Minister of Defence, regards the possibility of the *Bismarck* and *Prinz Eugen* – another new vessel, also swift and well-armed – loose in 'the great spaces of the Atlantic Ocean' as subjecting British 'naval strength to a trial of the first magnitude'.

–

Royal Navy warships with names that have become legends will soon be drawn into the pursuit of the

Bismarck. The *Ark Royal*, *Rodney*, *Dorsetshire*, and *Cossack* are exemplars of the massive maritime power the British can still draw on, showing a resilience and determination the Germans fear. Aboard those vessels are young men either in their teens or barely out of them, but who already know the rigours and risks of war.

HMS *Cossack*

Ken Robinson is an 18-year-old rating from the northwest of England and one of 219 men serving in the 2,519-ton destroyer HMS *Cossack*. In August 1939, he was working as a labourer and a bit bored with his lot. With war likely, he decided to join up, picking the Navy because its recruiting office was the easiest for him to get to. Robinson soon found himself on the way to the naval barracks at Portsmouth for basic training, joining the *Cossack* in January 1940. A sleek, fast warship, *Cossack*'s job is to scout ahead and provide protection for bigger vessels, whether they be waddling battleships or heavily-laden merchant vessels.

The *Cossack* is one of 16 Tribal Class ships – all named after famously warlike tribes – built for the Royal Navy in the late 1930s as Britain rearmed in the face of the growing German threat. With a principal armament of eight 4.7-inch guns and four tubes for

21-inch torpedoes, the *Cossack* also has depth charges and anti-aircraft guns.

The Royal Navy's destroyers are trouble-shooters who have already suffered heavily, used for suicidal attacks on enemy capital ships, to tackle enemy destroyers and sink U-boats. They paid a heavy price at the hands of enemy dive-bombers while evacuating troops from Dunkirk in May 1940. The fact that eleven of the Tribals will be sunk between April 1940 and September 1942 indicates their expendable nature and the risks they habitually take, sacrificing themselves to save others.

Even though he is not yet out of his teens, Robinson has been bloodied in several actions already, including a pitched battle on 13 April 1940 between British and German destroyers in the fjords around Narvik in Norway. He was a loader on the *Cossack*'s X-turret of two 4.7-inch guns, mounted aft in the ship.

> 'It was very, very fierce. The guns were firing more or less non-stop. The barrels were flippin' red hot. There were that many inlets of the fjord and the enemy destroyers had gone into different places. We went in after one in Narvik harbour. We passed through where another one had been sunk at the mouth of

the harbour, sailing right through survivors shouting for help. We couldn't stop and, as we entered, we were hit, but then we opened fire.

'I didn't know we had been really severely damaged until the end. There was only one hurt on X-turret, and he was hit by shrapnel. I suppose I was scared, but you were more frightened of showing it than anything else.

'We were quite busy, and then, after it was over, we were aground. Sailors from this German ship that was sunk on the other side of us must have gone ashore with rifles, because whilst Cossack was aground, they were firing from behind trees.

'Then a bit later a shell just dropped alongside Cossack — we heard the whistle and saw the spout in the water. We looked up and there was this gun on a lorry or a trailer or something, on a hillside. The Gunnery Officer himself came to X-turret because we were one of the guns that could still be fired. We'd lost power training, so it had to be done by hand. The Gunnery Officer trained it, went to the other side, sat in that chair, laid it and then to trainer's side and then fired. Anyway, it vanished, so I am sure we hit it.'

After the fight at Narvik, Robinson helped commit slain shipmates to the deep.

> 'The bodies had been sewn up in hammocks with weights inside and placed on narrow platforms – like planks – that would normally be lowered over the side for sailors to sit on to paint the ship. The firing party would fire and then we'd lift up these platforms and the bodies would slide off into the water. I didn't think too deeply about it at the time – it was happening to all the other ships, too, so it wasn't just us taking casualties. Really it is only since the war that I give it a lot of thought.'

At the beginning of the next year, the *Cossack* was sent to ride shotgun on the legendary *Hood*, which Robinson stared at with admiring eyes, reassured by her substantial presence.

> 'The *Hood* was beautiful, was our pride. When we look at the *Hood*, we think nothing can happen to us. We were the screen for the *Hood*, her protection from submarines.'

Ken nearly lost his life in heavy seas the mighty *Hood* just shrugged off.

'I was one of a detail trying to secure one of the whalers in davits on the deck. It was being washed away, so a Petty Officer came onto the mess deck and said: "You and you come with me."

'Altogether there were four of us and as we were lashing the boat down, he sent one man for another heaving line down in the tiller flat, at the stern of the ship.

'He didn't want to go, and the PO said: "You'll be alright, just keep hold of the lifeline as you go along the upper deck."

'So he went and just after he'd gone a wave came in one side and went right over the ship. It hit us and I finished up right in the guardrails clinging on. I got up and another one hit me, sending me back in the same place. The Petty Officer and the other rating had gone. I was the only survivor. Somebody must have seen it from the bridge and when I went back to the mess deck the First Lieutenant came asking me questions. Then this chap turns up from the tiller flat who everybody thought was dead.'

By late May 1941, the *Cossack* and other ships of the 4th Destroyer Flotilla, under the command of the aggressive Captain Philip Vian, are escorting a troop ship convoy sailing from the Clyde. Early on the morning of 24 May, the hammer blow falls.

> *'The Bosun's Mate came 'round and said: "Attention is drawn to the noticeboard re the Hood." So we went crowding 'round the notice and saw that it read: "Hood was sunk at 06.00 this morning". We couldn't believe it, but, of course, we had to believe it in the end.'*

HMS *Rodney*

Also on convoy protection duty and heading out into the Atlantic, several hundred miles to the north-west of Ireland on 24 May is HMS *Rodney*, one of the 15 big gun capital ships that are a mark of front-rank power status for Britain. In a pre-nuclear world battleships matter, for they are the most destructive force on the planet, the ultimate status symbol and big stick to wave at a potential enemy. The only way to match an enemy battleship in a gunfight is with another battleship.

In some respects, though, the 40,000 tons *Rodney* is ill-suited to taking on the *Bismarck*. While powerfully armed and well protected, with 16-inch guns more powerful than the German battleship's, *Rodney* is much older – *Bismarck* was launched in 1939, while *Rodney* went down the slipway in 1925. The

British battleship is slower too (with a top speed of 22 knots against the German vessel's 30 knots). She also has a crack in her main armour deck created by a German bomb that penetrated the ship during combat off Norway in April 1940. Fortunately, it shattered without exploding. In May 1941. as she accompanies a convoy across the Atlantic, *Rodney* is carrying a large piece of armour plate to Boston in the USA to be used in a major refit that will include covering up the crack.

Prior to Boston she is to visit Halifax, Nova Scotia and drop off 500 passengers – mainly servicemen destined for training in Canada – who are crammed into the ship alongside her usual complement of 1,314.

The *Rodney* is escorting two troop ships during her transatlantic crossing, and for now stays with them in case the *Bismarck* comes their way.

Her Commanding Officer, Captain Frederick Dalrymple-Hamilton, has been keeping everybody aboard fully briefed on the events as they unfold, by making reports on the ship's internal broadcast system.

One of those listening intently early on 24 May is Royal Marine Len Nicholl, aged 20, manning one of *Rodney*'s 6-inch gun turrets. Plymouth born and bred, he is the first of his family to join the Royal

Marines, signing up in 1939 because he was eager to do something for his country. A brother had served in a cruiser in the 1930s but was later killed by Japanese bombing at Shanghai. Len's dad died when he was two years old, a merchant mariner who at one time sailed in the *Olympic*, sister ship to the *Titanic*.

Such a background is not uncommon in a seafaring nation like Britain. Nicholl is one of thousands of Royal Marines by tradition assigned to vessels across the Navy to bolster ships' companies and operate some of the weapons, such as the gun turret where he is now listening intently to the captain.

> 'He said the cruiser Norfolk had spotted these German ships trying to break through the Denmark Strait and was trailing them, shadowing them and that the Hood and Prince of Wales were taking up position to engage them. This was around about half past five in the morning, and we were closed up at defence stations ourselves. Around about six o'clock, we had another broadcast, and he mentioned that Hood had blown up. After the captain's broadcast a mate of mine says to me: "What does he mean the Hood has blown up?" I said I should imagine it's gone kaput.'

Nicholl feels the loss of the battle-cruiser deeply.

'I had quite a number of friends on the Hood that went down with her, chaps that joined up with me.'

At his action station atop *Rodney*'s towering bridge structure is 19-year-old Midshipman Yves Dias, the battleship's Second Torpedo Officer. He knows only too well what it's like to be a victim of the enemy.

In December 1939, as a young apprentice Merchant Navy officer, he sailed in the oil tanker *San Alberto*, headed for Tampico on the Gulf of Mexico. She was attacked by *U-48* to the southwest of Ireland, and Dias was among those left aboard a gradually sinking vessel.

They were eventually saved after a passing merchant vessel noticed a distress signal. Once notified, the Admiralty sent a destroyer to save Dias and his shipmates. With no lifeboats, they were forced to jump into the sea and swim for their lives to a raft that was then hauled to the warship.

After recovering from the *San Alberto* ordeal, a few more trips in oil tankers followed, fortunately avoiding the attentions of enemy submarines or surface raiders. Then, Dias was taken into the Royal Navy, with his destination after training the *Rodney*.

HMS *Ark Royal*

If *Rodney* represents the past, the aircraft carrier, even if its full potential has yet to be demonstrated in war, is the future.

HMS *Ark Royal* is Britain's first truly modern ship of the type, carrying torpedo-bombers and fighter aircraft. When working with battleships, a carrier's job is to scout for enemy warships, to attack them, if necessary, and also to counter hostile air forces and submarines.

The Germans have nothing like the 27,000 tons the *Ark*, for, if there is one glaring weakness in their fleet, it is a total lack of carrier capability. They have launched just one such a ship – the *Graf Zeppelin* – but the head of the Luftwaffe, Herman Goering, is reluctant to let his aviators go to sea. There are also problems with fitting some of her equipment, so she will actually never be completed.

The Nazi propaganda machine has, since war broke out, claimed the *Ark*'s sinking several times, but she is still in the game, and now part of Force H, the Royal Navy's Gibraltar-based striking group. Her primary mission in May 1941 is escorting convoys to the besieged island of Malta and carrying out air raids with her Swordfish biplanes on Italian ports and other targets.

Among the *Ark*'s aviators is a 21-year-old Canadian, Terry Goddard, who has already had his share of brushes with death. Aside from seeing action in the skies over Narvik – trying and failing to bomb the same destroyers Ken Robinson's ship would fight – Goddard has evaded being shot down by enemy fighter aircraft over the English Channel. He was not so lucky in the Mediterranean.

> *'During one bombing attack on Cagliari, my Swordfish got heavily damaged. We decided we could make it back, but we ditched about 120 miles from the fleet. I got out a good Mayday and nine-and-a-half hours later, lo and behold, the destroyer HMS Foxhound came bursting over the horizon. She went steaming on by at full speed, which was a very sad moment. Then, suddenly, there was a big belch of black smoke and she shuddered around in the turn and came back. Incredibly, a cook who was throwing waste over the side reported to the bridge that he thought he saw something yellow in the water, [Goddard's dinghy] and that's how we were sighted.'*

Other than that, the Mediterranean at this time is a comparatively pleasant place to fight a war, especially against the Italians who possess none of the fanatical love of death or glory of the Germans.

> *'Force H was a really happy force. We ate well, we drank well, and we slept at night and had no idea of the distress of England.'*

There was, though, some unpleasantness when Britain was forced to attack the French fleet at Oran in North Africa, to prevent it falling into German hands after the surrender of France. Goddard and his fellow Swordfish aviators found themselves carrying out their first torpedo attack on a battleship that not long before was a friend. The *Strasbourg* had broken out of the Algerian naval base to escape a British bombardment led by HMS *Hood* and was making for Toulon.

> *'It was comical affair. Our performance was pretty abysmal, dropping torpedoes too far out, beyond the French destroyer screen. Strasbourg opened fire on us, but her firepower was not too great, and I don't think they shot at us with any great feeling.'*

The Germans are a different matter – in battle they mean it and mistakes against them are often fatal, as the *Hood* had discovered. As the routine of runs to

Malta carry on, the men of the *Ark Royal* have no inkling of facing anyone but the Italians.

> 'We got back to the Rock [Gibraltar] on 23 May after flying off some Hurricanes to Malta and we expected to stay in harbour for a while. We were advised we wouldn't be taking part in operations to counter the German invasion of Crete. At 2.30 in the morning on 24 May, we were woken up by the rock, rattle, and roll of the ship and the shuddering of the props, and we realised something was happening. I assumed we were off up the Med again. The next morning it was clear that we weren't. We were steaming west into a very unkind Atlantic. We then heard we were going to provide coverage for a convoy carrying 20,000 troops. The brand-new carrier Victorious and battle-cruiser Repulse had been withdrawn from escorting it to go and look for Bismarck, which we then heard was on the loose. About an hour later, or thereabouts, we got the news that Hood had been blown up. It was very traumatic, distressing, wretched news. The feeling of sorrow for all the people lost didn't sink in immediately. I think the basic feeling was one of anger. Anger that Hood

hadn't distinguished herself, for she was our pride and joy. Anger that the German gunnery was obviously so much better than ours. Anger that the Prince of Wales had retreated, and anger, I guess, that Bismarck was now loose in the Atlantic and that we had to find and sink her.'

KM *Bismarck*

Meanwhile, to the southeast of Greenland, the cruisers *Suffolk* and *Norfolk*, along with the damaged *Prince of Wales*, continue to shadow *Bismarck* and *Prinz Eugen*, occasionally venturing close and exchanging fire.

Vice Admiral Günther Lütjens, who as Fleet Commander, is leading the raiding mission (called Operation Rheinübung), decides it is pointless shackling *Prinz Eugen* with the job of accompanying *Bismarck* and sets her free early on the evening of 24 May by ordering the battleship to turn on her shadowers. During an exchange of fire, the German heavy cruiser disappears into the night.

In the early hours of 25 May, Swordfish torpedo-bombers from the *Victorious* carry out a gallant attack on the Bismarck. The British aircraft is deceptively antiquated looking. Though a biplane that chugs through the air sounding like an aerial tractor, the

Swordfish is not that old, having entered Fleet Air Arm service in 1937.

Affectionately nicknamed the 'Stringbag' – because it can carry just about any weapon – the Swordfish won its spurs in late 1940 by knocking out Italian battleships in Taranto harbour. The first U-boat sunk in the Second World War by the British was courtesy of a Swordfish using bombs. It is as a torpedo-bomber that the Swordfish will achieve new fame in May 1941.

It has a crew of three tucked into its long, narrow open cockpit – a pilot, a navigator (or Observer in Royal Navy parlance), and a rating Telegraphist Air Gunner (TAG) whose job is sending and receiving Morse code signals and operating the rear-facing machine gun.

The Swordfish is an unlikely saviour and not many would bet on its chances of success, not least the battleship advocates who disdain naval aviators and their puny aircraft. Slow, with only a top speed of 138 mph, its two wings do give it incredible lift. A monoplane needs around 30 knots of wind across the flight-deck to take off from a carrier, but a Swordfish can take off from a vessel at anchor (and even into the teeth of gale).

Constructed from wood, canvas and metal struts, the Swordfish can survive hits that will destroy metal skinned aircraft, for the simple reason that cannon shells and bullets pass right through it.

When the *Bismarck's* gunners tried to shoot down the Swordfish of 825 Squadron, they found it extremely tricky to even hit them. Not only were they flying slower than *Bismarck's* anti-aircraft guns were calibrated for, they even crabbed sideways and seemed to tumble up and down like leaves.

For all its wonderfully eccentric survival attributes, it still takes a brave man to fly a Swordfish, indeed any aircraft, against the heavily armed *Bismarck*. One plucky 825 Squadron pilot, Sub Lieutenant Pat Jackson, remarks of his torpedo run against the German battleship:

> *'The Bismarck of course was taking evasive action and so it was quite difficult to gauge how far ahead one should aim with the rudimentary gauge that we had for this… However, once a torpedo's gone, you don't hang around and you're out of it as quick as you can.'*

As he made his escape, Jackson had to be careful that a near miss did not knock the aircraft out of the sky.

> *'I think she [Bismarck] was firing some very heavy armament because these shells were coming down, raising very large columns of*

> *water which would have been fatal if you flew into them.'*

—

Shock damage caused by the single torpedo hit achieved during the 825 Squadron attack kills a sailor and causes even more flooding in *Bismarck*'s Port Boiler Room 2. Violent manoeuvring needed to evade the other torpedoes dislodges collision mats put in place to seal the holes in the bow, letting in water. *Bismarck*'s speed is slowed down to 16 knots.

Even this cannot dampen the feeling in *Bismarck* that she is doing well.

However, Lütjens decides to temper the joy of those under his command.

Using the public address system, the admiral salutes the discipline of *Bismarck*'s men and commends them on their dutiful performance, but he warns that the entire enemy fleet will be hunting them, 'to sink the killer of the *Hood*'.

Now Lütjens explains they must 'win or die', and, if sunk, they will ensure many of the enemy are destroyed in the process. This indicates the deeply fatalistic outlook he has privately nurtured on how the mission will turn out. Even before the *Bismarck* began her sortie, the admiral confessed to a friend:

'I shall not return. Considering British [naval] superiority, survival is unlikely.'

In the opinion of engineering officer, Kapitänleutnant Gerhard Junack, the admiral goes too far in sharing his pessimism with the battleship's men. While he may have aimed to 'rid the crew of over-exuberance and bring them into a more realistic frame of mind ... he overdid it, and there was a feeling of depression' across the entire crew and a feeling of doom. *Bismarck*'s men 'began to brood and neglected their duties'.

A plan for the *Bismarck* to lead the pursuing British into a U-boat ambush also begins to come apart at the seams. This is a bitter blow.

Lütjens, in April 1941, had convened a planning meeting in Paris with Rear Admiral Karl Dönitz, the U-boat force boss. The old friends discussed how they might coordinate the battleship's operations with submarines to inflict pain on enemy convoys and even on the British navy. Such a one-two tactic had been used with mixed results in March 1941. Back then, when the battlecruisers *Gneisenau* and *Scharnhorst* found a battleship escorting a convoy, instead of attacking, they held off and provided directions for U-boats. This enabled submarines to get in among the long lines of slow merchant vessels and cause havoc with torpedo attacks. That was how convoy SL-67 lost five merchant ships on 8 March, sunk by *U-124* and *U-105*, off the Cape Verde Islands.

For that earlier sortie, it had been agreed by the German naval leadership that, should a U-boat damage an escorting British battleship, the *Gneisenau* or *Scharnhorst* would then seek to ravage the British convoy.

U-106 attacked convoy SL-68 on 20 March 1941: a torpedo hit was scored on the elderly battlewagon HMS *Malaya* – forcing her to withdraw, heavily damaged, and head for repairs in Trinidad. However, the *Gneisenau* and *Scharnhorst* failed to take advantage of the situation.

As a result of that missed opportunity, during their April meeting, Dönitz and Lütjens agreed a veteran submarine officer would be embarked in *Bismarck* to help coordinate joint efforts with patrolling U-boats during Operation Rheinübung. This would be done via wireless signals between the *Bismarck* and the U-boat Force headquarters in France, which would then move its pieces around on the Atlantic chessboard to try to arrange an ambush.

On 24 May, Dönitz offered to order his U-boats to cease their operations against enemy convoys in order to assist *Bismarck* and *Prinz Eugen*. This, however, scored a silent victory for Britain, which gained temporary relief from U-boat attacks.

Lütjens asked for U-boats to be positioned to the south of Greenland. But he was then forced – due to loss of oil caused by the *Prince of Wales* 14-inch shell hit on the fuel tank – to take the *Bismarck* south and southeast. This was away from the ambush location, but a more direct course for a port on the French Atlantic coast to receive dockyard repairs. Observing this by studying the latest information on the plot at his headquarters, Dönitz ordered a patrol line of U-boats to be established in the Bay of Biscay, hoping to stage an ambush of British warships there.

–

Though many ships are on the lookout, catastrophe strikes for the British in the early hours of 25 May when, using poor visibility amid sleet and mountainous seas, the *Bismarck* slips the hounds on her trail.

There are fears in London that the enemy raiders will either destroy a vital convoy or return in triumph to Germany where the *Hood*'s destruction will be celebrated, ensuring Britain's humiliation is complete. The world will also think the Royal Navy is incapable of safeguarding Atlantic lifelines, never mind protecting the empire.

Finding and destroying *Bismarck* is paramount. There is surely not much time left to catch her before she comes under the protective umbrella of the Luftwaffe and German warships reach her to provide an escort to a safe harbour. The next 24 hours will be crucial in deciding whether the *Bismarck* slips the grasp of the British or meets her doom.

26 May

8.40AM: Weather report for area within 200 miles of 50° N., 20° W. – Strong Northwest wind slowly slackening – backing in West – cloudy – squall – occasional showers – visibility 8–12 miles.

—Signal from the Admiralty to Ships of
the Home Fleet

Seeking a ship in the vastness of the Atlantic Ocean – even one as big as the *Bismarck* – is even harder than looking for a needle in a haystack.

The German battleship is a fast-moving target in a boundless sea and so easily missed. Yet, with eyes in the sky and lookouts scanning the horizon from the crow's nests of various ships, there is still a slim chance of success.

10.30 am – *Bismarck* Where Art Thou?

The Nazi raider has been lost for 31 hours, with much of the British fleet searching in the wrong direction –

north – as the *Bismarck* still heads southeast, making for the Atlantic coast of German-occupied France.

The Germans make the error of underestimating the wireless signal interception, interpretation, and code-breaking capabilities of the British. The continual sending of wireless messages by the *Bismarck* to naval headquarters, and also to Hitler (27 in all by Admiral Lütjens across the course of the Action), is a massive blunder.

The use by the Kriegsmarine of wireless signals between vessels and their shore-based headquarters to coordinate long-range operations, whether by capital ships or submarines, can be a tremendous advantage – for example, in assembling U-boat wolf packs to attack Allied convoys – but is also an Achilles heel.

This is because the Royal Navy's at-sea wireless specialists can gain considerable intelligence just by studying the locality and duration of German wireless traffic. Meanwhile, Direction Finding (DF) stations ashore can coordinate their efforts, in order to plot fixes for the locations of U-boats and surface raiders blurting out wireless signals, the longer the better.

Early on the morning of 25 May, due to flawed DF fixes by shore stations in the UK, the *Bismarck* did catch a break.

The Admiralty's Operational Intelligence Centre (OIC) in London correctly plotted the *Bismarck* heading south and east, but, rather than send this correct analysis, raw data from the UK-based DF stations was conveyed to the Home Fleet flagship, the battleship HMS *King George V*. It was therefore calculated in the *King George V* that the enemy was going in the opposite direction, hence the fleet headed north when it should have gone south. Had the DF station at Gibraltar also detected the *Bismarck*'s signals and plotted them, confirmation that she was heading south rather than north may have been achieved.

–

But, if the magic of DF temporarily failed, the 'Mark One Eyeball' – on 26 May someone's acute vision – saves the day. A Catalina flying boat of the RAF, acting on information from the OIC – which persists in its view that *Bismarck* is heading south and east – has been searching a particular box of sea and finds a mystery warship, around 690 miles to the west of Brest. The Catalina sends a sighting report at 10.30 am:

> *One battleship latitude 49° 33' N., 21° 47' W., course 150°, speed 20.*

An encrypted Luftwaffe message has also been cracked by a code breaker at Bletchley Park, which indicates the *Bismarck* is indeed heading for Brest. Some of the British warships at sea are making moves to cover that eventuality anyway, not least HMS *Rodney*.

Force H is already in place, having been ordered by the Admiralty on 25 May to place itself to block a clear run by the *Bismarck* to Brest or St Nazaire, just in case. That precaution was predicated on the logic that the *Bismarck* would join the *Gneisenau* and *Scharnhorst* (then lurking in Brest after their spring foray into the Atlantic).

Keeping *Bismarck* away from these other German ships is crucial for the British: if the Germans later send all three out on a combined sortie with the elusive *Prinz Eugen*, that will mean big trouble for Atlantic convoys.

On the morning of 26 May, stopping the *Bismarck* in her tracks still seems a rather tall order. HMS *King George V* is 130 miles to the north of *Bismarck*, and, while the *Rodney* is nearer, she is of course old and slow compared to the German battleship.

10.51 am – Request a Check

HMS *King George V*

Relief that contact has been renewed soon turns to fear that it may not have been the *Bismarck* found, but rather a British vessel.

Home Fleet commander Admiral Jack Tovey, in HMS *King George V*, breaks radio silence to signal the Admiralty 21 minutes later:

> *The Catalina 1030 contact report – Request a check that contact was not RODNEY…*

Before confirmation can be provided, the Catalina reveals it has lost contact. The flying boat resumes the search, desperately trying to catch sight of the mystery battleship through breaks in the cloud.

HMS *Ark Royal*

In the meantime, the Force H carrier force is steaming hard to the rescue having, on orders of the Admiralty, abandoned the convoy escort task. Brave words about tackling *Bismarck* – perhaps said while secretly hoping it won't come to that – will now be put to the test. 'Obviously protecting merchant ships had been the Admiralty's top priority,' reflects Terry Goddard, 'and covering a convoy was a nice light-hearted duty for us, though a bit dicey with the bad weather.'

'That feeling of complacency was very rapidly changed when we suddenly altered course. The destroyers were sent back to Gib and we went north at maximum possible speed.'

When the *Victorious* launched her attack on the *Bismarck* the previous day, the Germans failed to shoot any aircraft down, but British aviators had still been killed. The crews of some Fulmar fighters launched by the carrier to find and shadow *Bismarck* lost their way and didn't make it back to the ship – the homing beacon of the *Victorious* was not working. The lost aircraft ditched and most of the aviators died of exposure or drowned. Naval flyers, including Goddard, often feel their own side is their worst enemy.

'Those Fulmars shouldn't have been sent out on shadowing. Their radios and compasses were not working when they were launched and on a mission for which the aircraft type was not suited. There was no adequate lighting in the rear cockpit and the Fulmar's exhaust flare wiped out any forward vision. Even with compasses and radios that worked, the Fulmar was not suited for night reconnaissance and shadowing.'

The *Ark*'s aviators do not fancy their chances if they also have to ditch.

> *'We now had no plane guard – no destroyer to pull us out of the drink if our aircraft crashed into the sea. If you ditched, you were gone.'*

Despite the stormy weather, the *Ark Royal* – with Force H by then approximately 75 miles to the east of the *Bismarck* – launches Swordfish to try and find *Bismarck*. Goddard's aircraft is among those sent off to seek out the German battleship.

> *'Ark Royal lurched into wind. Finally, it was our turn. Lumbered slowly up a flight deck that was more like a hill, with the Swordfish airborne as it passed the ship's island. We spotted some guy holding up a blackboard with a revised Ark Royal position, so we could find our way back. Once airborne, thoughts of toppling or flying into the ocean were soon displaced by how to best carry out the search. Decided it was best to get above the muck. At about 5,000 feet, we found a window between top of muck and bottom of towering cumulus. Agreed to stay there. I always took care to get the homing beacon fine-tuned. Thoughts now turned to Bismarck and what she might*

look like. No breaks in the muck below us.
After about 15 minutes it was agreed we should
get below it. Visibility remained lousy. Air
unstable – bumpy with showers – miserable
and really unpleasant. Then, without warning
or expectation we were in the clear – no cloud –
calmer seas with good visibility. Sweating and
dry mouth ease up.'

11.14 am – Contact!

While Goddard's Swordfish fails to find the *Bismarck*,
another one – likewise equipped with Air-to-Surface
Vessel (ASV) radar – does, reporting to *Ark Royal*:

> *One enemy battleship 292°, 83 miles from 49°*
> *N., 19° W.*

Almost simultaneously, the RAF Catalina discovers
the *Bismarck* again, dipping below cloud to be greeted
with a storm of fire and signalling:

> *Hull holed by shrapnel*

The chase is back on, with Home Fleet flagship *King
George V* and the *Rodney* making adjustments to their
courses – the former turning south and putting on
maximum speed. The captain of the latter tries to
guess where to position his ship in order to block the

Bismarck's route to her most likely destination, which is reckoned to be Brest.

11.30 am – Breaking Radio Silence

HMS *Dorsetshire*

Way off to the south, another warship commander has been devouring the signals and decides to let the Admiralty know he is well placed.

'Intend to leave convoy now,' Captain Benjamin Martin, aboard the heavy cruiser *Dorsetshire*, signals, 'steer 65, speed 25, to intercept and shadow the enemy. I have 59% fuel on hand.'

The Admiralty does not object, wanting to keep direct exchanges of signals between itself and units to a minimum.

It also recognises that Capt Martin is doing what is expected of him.

Since the days of Nelson, the commanders of British warships have, when possible, tried to follow the famous admiral's dictum:

> *No captain can do very wrong if he places his ship alongside that of the enemy.*

As a cruiser, the *Dorsetshire*'s function since joining the front-line fleet in the early 1930s has been to police the empire, showing the flag to make friends and influence people, also putting ashore armed landing parties to quell rebellions if need be, and using her eight 8-inch guns to bombard them into submission as a last resort. Designed to cruise vast distances between Britain and imperial possessions around the globe, the 10,000 tons ship can manage an impressive 32 knots.

It is escort work that she is currently mainly employed in, and the *Dorsetshire*'s presence on a convoy, rushing around at speed like a protective sheepdog rounding up merchant vessels, guarantees a measure of safety for ships carrying trade that is the lifeblood of Britain and the empire.

Cruisers are also useful supporting players to capital ships in any battle, dividing the enemy's fire, doing whatever additional damage they can with their guns and torpedoes. Prior to battle they can shadow the opposition and broadcast the target's location – via encrypted wireless signals – to the Admiralty and friendly capital ships, as the *Norfolk* and *Suffolk* are now doing with *Bismarck*.

Standing by Capt Martin's side aboard the *Dorsetshire* as he decides to leave the convoy to assist in the *Bismarck* pursuit, is 17-year-old Boy Sailor George Bell. From a Cumbrian farming family, Bell always fancied a life at sea. Prior to entering the Service, he received an introduction to naval life aboard the *Warspite*, a former cruiser of the Victorian navy turned floating school moored on the Thames and run by the Marine Society charity. As the Captain's messenger, Bell is answerable directly to the CO of *Dorsetshire*. He must do only the Captain's bidding. Barefoot for better grip on the deck, he takes important messages to different parts of the ship. Throughout the whole Action, except when carrying messages, Bell will always be close to the compass platform from where Capt Martin commands the vessel.

> 'In the year I served as Captain Martin's messenger, I never ever saw him go outside shouting distance of the bridge. He had an office with a bunk put in it and even that was within six yards of the compass platform. He had a proper sea cabin with a shower that he used to go down to occasionally. Otherwise he never left that bridge and was always within hailing distance of the officer of the watch. If there was ever an alarm on the bridge, he would be there very, very quickly.
>
> 'On this occasion he told us what Dorsetshire was doing over the public address system and we were rather surprised and thought: "Gosh if Bismarck does come our way what

chance have we got?" Even so, the last thing we wanted was to allow Bismarck under any circumstances to stay out and cause havoc to our convoys.

'I think the first thing in Captain Martin's mind was to protect his own convoy, which he could do by stopping Bismarck if she decided to go south. We didn't know what state Bismarck was in, or even what kind of British fleet there was chasing her. We knew the Hood had been sunk and that Bismarck was on the loose.'

11.45 am – Bad News for German Headquarters

KM *Bismarck*

Admiral Lütjens dictates a signal telling naval HQ in northern France that biplanes have been spotted. This indicates an enemy aircraft carrier is close. *Bismarck's* anti-aircraft guns spit fire at the shadowing Swordfish without effect – the British planes hang on.

12.00 Noon – Handing Over the Baton

The Swordfish tasked with keeping an eye on the *Bismarck* are being run in relay, with a fresh pair launched from *Ark Royal* at noon.

One of them is Swordfish A2M, commanded by 24-year-old Lieutenant (Observer) John Lang, who has already seen action in the Mediterranean and Norwegian campaign, and his pilot is Sub Lieutenant FR 'Steve' Crabbe.

To give the Swordfish range and endurance in the reconnaissance role, an auxiliary fuel tank is strapped into the long cockpit behind the pilot. Lang is squashed in beside it, coping with both the freezing wind and also trying to operate the wireless set.

It is a most uncomfortable experience, with the petrol tank pushing against Lang's back, the radio nudging his knees and 'a vent to the petrol tank pushing out nasty smelly petrol fumes'.

The first indication they have found the *Bismarck* is the Swordfish nearly colliding with the RAF Catalina already shadowing the enemy vessel. It is rather drily described by Lang as follows:

> *'We met the RAF flying boat at fairly close quarters in a cloud and parted quickly.'*

The job now is to stay in visual contact with the *Bismarck*, sending coded wireless messages containing the position and heading of the German ship.

Bismarck appears to be down at the bows and leaking a trail of oil, which is gleaming on the sea. Otherwise, Lang thinks the *Bismarck* looks like 'the most magnificent ship' as he peers down over the side of the cockpit, the Swordfish flying 'across the stern or across the bows'.

Whenever the Swordfish gets too close, the *Bismarck*'s anti-aircraft guns sparkle angrily, with shells bursting close to the enemy plane in shrapnel-laced puffs of black smoke. Lt Crabbe veers the Swordfish away momentarily and then edges back over the enemy vessel.

12.30 pm – The Worst Days Yet

Having spent a desperately anxious weekend at his Chequers country retreat – kept constantly up-dated with the latest news on the *Bismarck* breakout and other events by the Admiralty – Winston Churchill heads back to London by car at high speed.

The loss of the *Hood*, the massive German para-trooper assault on Crete, and failure to yet sink the *Bismarck* have been, in the PM's view the worst three days of the war yet. He is to hold a War Cabinet meeting to consider the *Bismarck* situation. Churchill is not yet aware that contact has been renewed with the German battleship.

12.45 pm – Vian's Dash

HMS *Cossack*

Capt Vian is also reading signals and coming to a decision.

In the early hours of 26 May he was ordered by the Admiralty to make a rendezvous with the *King George V* to provide escort, as her own destroyers were soon to withdraw due to lack of fuel.

Vian decides he will not do that after all.

He deduces that he should take his ships – in addition to the *Cossack*, the 4th Destroyer Flotilla is composed of the *Zulu*, *Maori*, *Sikh* and the Polish destroyer *Piorun* – and head for where he judges the German battleship will be. Vian thinks the *Bismarck* will head for a port in the Bay of Biscay. Sending the flotilla in that direction will place him near *King George V* anyway.

But the flotilla's dash proves far from easy in dreadful seas that threaten to overwhelm the destroyers as they batter their way south. Engines straining, their fuel is gobbled up by the effort. Sometimes their screws thrash thin air as their sterns are lifted out of the water.

Conditions at sea for the destroyer men are tough at the best of times. Ken Robinson thinks the *Cossack* 'definitely a special ship' but living in her can some-times be a terrible experience.

> *'It wasn't comfortable, especially in the North Atlantic. We were always tired, constantly cold, never getting a night's sleep in a hammock unless we came into harbour. If you were lucky you stayed overnight. At sea a favourite place to sleep was on top of the lockers, which were on one side of the messdeck table. On the other side was a long stool, which was a bit narrow. With experience, you managed to sleep on it, unless it was that rough you just fell off. Even on the lockers you'd wake up and the table would have collapsed. The mess deck would be full of water and the lockers lifted off their mountings and floating about and you'd be soaking wet. That was regular, but we didn't sleep in hammocks at sea because it would take too long to get dressed if the action stations alarm sounded off. The instructions were to sleep fully dressed and near the defence station.'*

Having endured days of this exhausting existence, the spirits of the men are lifted by the thought of action. The *Cossack* seems to be in the thick of it no matter where she is.

Innes Hamilton is the destroyer's 24-year-old first lieutenant, or 'Number One', who has already seen quite a bit of action.

The son of an army officer, who was badly wounded at Gallipoli during the First World War, Innes was born in Dunbar, Scotland. He attended Britannia Royal Naval College, Dartmouth as boy and, while not a great sportsman, excelled in the classroom. By 1938, he was the youngest Lieutenant in the Royal Navy.

Hamilton joined the *Maori* before she was even completed at Govan in the Fairfields Yard, on the Clyde, starting as the gunnery officer.

It was when the *Maori* was in Alexandria Harbour with the Mediterranean Fleet that her captain cleared lower deck on 3 September 1939 and revealed to Hamilton and the rest of the crew:

'Gentlemen, we are at war.'

The *Maori* returned to home waters with the rest of the 4th Destroyer Flotilla. By May 1940, when Norway finally yielded to German invaders after months of fighting, Hamilton and the *Maori* were at Namsos evacuating Allied troops. Hamilton remembers:

> '...the remains of our army straggled down the
> beach in total disarray ... the German aircraft
> [were] strafing civilians as they climbed the
> mountains to get away from the air raids ...
> we were the last ship to leave.'

The destroyer itself was damaged by enemy bombs:
20 of the *Maori*'s sailors were wounded, and five
later died. After repairs, the *Maori* re-joined the 4th
Destroyer Flotilla, which switched to the Western
Approaches Command, operating out of Plymouth.

–

As the *Maori* and Vian's other destroyers steam at high
speed towards the *Bismarck*, bows slicing through the
waves – Hamilton is reading Admiralty signals and
studying the ship's Atlantic chart. He realises that he
has a front seat for one of history's great moments.

> 'The Bismarck Action – taking a broad
> view – represented the last time probably
> that destroyers performed their traditional role,
> which was to find the enemy ... The destroyers
> should lay off and not be sunk themselves, but
> continuously report the position of the enemy
> so that our heavy force could meet up with the
> enemy and so on ... the whole Atlantic was

one huge plot of ships all aiming to detect the
Bismarck and to bring her to action with our
heavy ships.'

1.10 pm – Tension at the War Rooms

Despite news of regained contact with *Bismarck*, the
mood in the Cabinet War Rooms bunker in White-
hall is very dark – Churchill asks what will happen if
the British ships now run out of fuel? The Black Dog
of gnawing depression is upon him, and he foresees
a very awkward announcement to the nation – that
the killer of the *Hood* has escaped retribution.

1.30 pm – The Old Girl Seeks

HMS *Rodney*

Already heading southeast to intercept *Bismarck*'s anti-
cipated track, the *Rodney* is battling against defective
engines but somehow steams on.

Capt Dalrymple-Hamilton convenes a meeting of
his Operations Committee. This is a group of his
most senior officers, all blessed with good tactical
sense. They consider how best to preserve fuel
while seeking to rendezvous with the rest of the
British fleet. Some excitement is provided when an
enemy Condor reconnaissance aircraft pops out of the

clouds, with the *Rodney* and her escorting destroyers firing at it but failing to score any hits.

As his ship ploughs on, Len Nicholl has time to ponder the last time he saw an enemy high seas commerce raider, which was as recently as March 1941. The *Rodney* caught one in the act of destroying a ship carrying a cargo of bacon from Newcastle to Newfoundland.

> *'We had trouble with the heavy cruiser Gneisenau and battlecruiser Scharnhorst in late 1940 and early 1941. They were sinking ships ten a penny. We picked up some of the crew of the Chilean Reefer, which was sunk by Gneisenau.'*

Rodney held her fire because she couldn't correctly identify the vessel looming behind the *Chilean Reefer*.

> *'Gneisenau was in the dark sky, in the east, and we were in the west with the setting sun behind us. She could easily have had a go at us, but she didn't.'*

The British battleship flashed a challenge via a signal light:

> *What Ship?*

The other vessel replied:

HMS Emerald.

A British cruiser. Taking advantage of the confusion, *Gneisenau* withdrew into the dark.

> *'By the time we got to the Chilean Reefer she was burning quite well. We picked up a few of their survivors. Two of them had died of exposure or injuries in the lifeboat we found. They thought they were being picked up by Gneisenau or the Scharnhorst. They didn't realise it was a British ship, but we got them aboard. The next day one of them came around the ship. He had a look at our turrets and said: "God if I had these guns I'd have sunk that [German] ship." Those merchant seamen were very brave lads.'*

The man who ordered the deceptive signal and then a retreat from the much more powerful *Rodney* was, of course, none other than Admiral Lütjens. Two months later he is now making life or death decisions for the *Bismarck* and her men. For *Rodney* – with contact maintained by aircraft – this time there is no doubt about ship identity.

But sometimes terrible mistakes are made, and Len Nicholl recalls an incident that illustrates well the problems of ship identity and the terror high seas raiders can inspire in the hearts of merchant mariners.

'We encountered a ship off Iceland one particular evening and sent them a signal asking
who they were. They wouldn't reply. So we
fired a 6-inch shell across their bows. Some of
the crew jumped over the side thinking they
were about to be slaughtered by one of these
German raiders. I suppose they got in a panic.
Up around that area you wouldn't be in the
water very long before you passed away due to
the cold. Once they found out who we were
they went back in to Halifax, Nova Scotia
where most of the crew came from. When we
went in there, they kicked us to death when we
went on shore leave. They were accusing us of
killing their men. Quite a few of the families
there took a very dim view of the Rodney.
It was a very treacherous time but also very
boring, travelling to and fro with convoys. You
were up and down the Atlantic, all the time at
sea and in bitter weather. And off the coast of
Canada it was invariably rough and misty as
well. Pretty grisly days really.'

In the minds of Rodney's sailors and marines there is, in late May 1941, a desire to avenge not only the Hood but also to hit back for their own families. The *Rodney* is a Devonport Division ship, manned by sailors and Royal Marines from Plymouth, the Devon naval port that hosts both a huge dockyard and naval base. Many of *Rodney*'s men have families and loved ones plunged into the cauldron of the war during several Luftwaffe fire bombing raids.

The most serious occurred in March and April 1941, wiping out the heart of the historic city. During Nicholl's time away in the *Rodney*, his family had been bombed out of their home in the Stonehouse district where the city's main Royal Marines barracks is to this day.

A residential block was hit with incendiary bombs that also set fire to a garage and its petrol tanks whose vent pipes were in the garden of the Nicholl family home. Luckily, everyone took cover in an Anderson shelter in the garden. Emerging later, they found their house had collapsed into its cellar. With his family going to live on Dartmoor to get away from the bombing, Nicholl asked for special leave.

'My family never even saved a spoon and didn't come back to Plymouth for 17 years. At the time, Rodney was at Scapa Flow, and people that, like myself, lived in Plymouth, especially married men, were getting compassionate leave. I wasn't married, but I put in for

leave anyway. The Captain said to me: "It's no use sending you down there. You haven't got a family other than your mum and dad. You're just an extra mouth to feed." So he didn't grant it, which is natural … it's not like I could do anything to help them out, really.'

There was no room for unnecessary sentiment in wartime, and sometimes those men that went home on compassionate leave were either killed in a subsequent air raid or simply deserted.

In the battle for control of the Atlantic, every man is needed in order do his duty, whether German or British. For the British navy, as the pursuit of *Bismarck* intensifies, all hands aboard every ship will be expected to play their parts in bringing things to a successful conclusion.

2.00 pm – Force H Prepares to Strike

Light signals flash between vessels, in this case a capital ship and a cruiser, one of the Royal Navy's long-range scouts. Sending messages between ships using lamps and a form of Morse code is a means of conversing with each other and not risking the enemy intercepting and decoding wireless transmissions. Using signal flags similarly preserves radio silence and keeps the foe in the dark about your intentions.

Therefore, from his flagship, the battlecruiser *Renown*, Admiral James Somerville orders the cruiser *Sheffield* ahead, to make visual contact with the German battleship.

HMS *Ark Royal*

Swordfish of 820 Squadron are prepared for a torpedo strike on the Nazi raider. One pilot, Lt Alan Swanton, vows:

> *'We aren't going to let Adolf get away with sinking Hood.'*

2.15 pm – Leaving the British Behind...

KM *Bismarck*

Kapitän Ernst Lindemann, the battleship's Commanding Officer, and Admiral Lütjens read a message from naval headquarters in France, detailing a Condor sighting report. It says the British battleship *Rodney* has been sighted but is at least 200 miles behind. The Germans fear *Rodney*'s 16-inch guns above all others but know her slow top speed means they can outrun her.

2.36 pm – Force Gathers

The Home Fleet

Lookouts in the *Rodney* spot *King George V* and vice versa. Admiral Tovey realises he now has the concentrated firepower necessary to destroy the *Bismarck* – if he can just catch up.

3.00 pm – A Comedy of Errors

Not far away, in a farcical episode, the *Ark Royal*'s Swordfish mistakenly attack *Sheffield*, which dodges the torpedoes, restraining her anti-aircraft gunners. Her captain and other members of the crew hurl abuse and shake fists at the aviators, who possibly thought she was the *Prinz Eugen*.

HMS *Cossack*

Fortunately for the destroyers in Vian's flotilla, also seeking out the *Bismarck* in the same locality, there is no way they can be mistaken for the enemy and attacked. The Kriegsmarine's destroyer force was devastated during the clash at Narvik in April 1940. Any surviving German destroyers lack the range to get that far out into the Atlantic.

Ken Robinson, at his new action station as the loader of a 2pdr pom-pom anti-aircraft weapon spots some black dots in the sky.

'There was nine Fairey Swordfish flying along. They were practically alongside us, flying and waving to us from the cockpits – I think it was those that fired on the Sheffield.'

HMS *Ark Royal*

Shortly before the bungled attack was launched, Terry Goddard touched down on completion of his shadowing mission. He had something to eat and then headed for his bunk to get some sleep. Terry is woken up by a rating who offers a mug of tea and news of the attack on *Sheffield*.

'So 820 Squadron takes off to attack Bismarck. The C-in-C [Admiral Tovey] not trusting the Swordfish to maintain contact with Bismarck, which actually they did, detached Sheffield. Ark's command didn't notice that Sheffield had been detached. The message stating Sheffield had been detached sits in the radio room. When 820 Squadron takes off they have no idea that Sheffield is up shadowing Bismarck. They pick up a bip on their radar and they attack the Sheffield. Now, for heaven's sake, the Sheffield is a two-stack 11,000 tons 8-inch gun cruiser, while Bismarck is a single stack [funnel], 50,000 tons battleship three

times the size of Sheffield, with 15-inch guns.
For whatever reason the torpedoes had been
armed with temperamental magnetic heads.
Fortunately for Sheffield the majority of the
torpedoes explode on hitting the water. She
manages to avoid the rest. Then they come
back to Ark. Of course Captain [Loben]
Maund, the Ark's CO, said there would be
no recriminations, but the rest of us thought it
was a pretty poor show.'

3.51 pm – Enemy Found

A Luftwaffe Condor long-range scout aircraft
discovers the Home Fleet, provoking a storm of
anti-aircraft fire. The *Bismarck* will now be told by
encoded wireless signal that the British fleet, not just
Rodney, is hot on her tail.

5.35 pm – Shadowers Return

HMS *Ark Royal*

With the *Sheffield* in visual contact with *Bismarck*, the
watch kept up by the *Ark*'s second pair of aircraft
has been stood down, though both Swordfish are
replaced by another two that will stay over the enemy
for as long as possible.

Returning safely to the carrier, after climbing down from his aircraft, and despite his extreme fatigue, Lt Lang offers to go back into the air for whatever attack on *Bismarck* is being arranged that evening. He is told by his friend, and 810 Squadron senior pilot, Lt David Godfrey-Faussett:

'John Lang, you have done enough.'

The Home Fleet

Light signals flash between the *Rodney* and *King George V*, as Tovey and Dalrymple-Hamilton discuss the looming battleship fuel crisis: they might run out before they can bring the *Bismarck* to battle.

Escorting destroyers are now pulling away to head back to a British port in order to refuel, removing the anti-submarine screen.

Where is Capt Vian with the destroyers of the 4th Flotilla?

5.40 pm – Proceeding with Caution

HMS *Sheffield*

A lookout on the cruiser's bridge spots the silhouette of the *Bismarck* on the horizon, coming south. The cruiser cautiously edges her way around north of the German battleship, staying out of range of the *Bismarck*'s guns, to take up a shadowing position.

5.47 pm – Not Worth the Bother

KM *Bismarck*

Lookouts in the German battleship scrutinise the dim shape of the *Sheffield* in the distance, but the decision is made to not bother opening fire.

Once again, a British cruiser trails the *Bismarck* while Swordfish scout planes loiter in the distance. Doom cannot be far away, unless *Bismarck* can shake them off.

The Berghof

Meanwhile, from his mountain retreat in Bavaria, Adolf Hitler puts in his second telephone call to Herman Göring since it became clear *Bismarck* is being hunted by enemy carriers.

Having already asked the Luftwaffe chief for an air attack on HMS *Victorious* after her 25 May attack on the *Bismarck*, Hitler now wants bombers to sink the *Ark Royal*.

He gets the same response: It cannot be done.

None of the available bombers based in France has the range or endurance for such a mission that far out into the Atlantic. Only the Condor maritime patrol aircraft could try and meet the challenge, but the Führer has previously ordered they should not be risked excessively.

5.58 pm – Running Out of Time… and Fuel

The Home Fleet

More light signals flash between the *King George V* and *Rodney*. Tovey tells Dalrymple-Hamilton he may have to turn around at midnight, as the speed with which the pursuit is being maintained is burning up too much oil The only hope is for Swordfish torpedo-bombers to damage *Bismarck* and slow her down, but can the *Ark Royal*'s aviators pull it off?

7.00 pm – The Next Bid to Stop *Bismarck*

HMS *Ark Royal*

It is time for another set of contenders to climb into the ring for a round with the heavyweight. The *Hood* had tried and was blown apart, the *Prince of Wales* was injured, and the flyers of the *Victorious* appeared not to have even bruised the Nazi behemoth during their Swordfish attack.

During the afternoon of 26 May *Ark*'s 820 Squadron had mistakenly attacked *Sheffield*.

Now 818 and 810 Squadrons are being called forward, asked to inflict some kind of decisive blow – maybe not landing a haymaker but enough to shatter one or two bones, to hobble the *Bismarck*.

As the *Ark* prepares to launch another strike, the underlying tension is severe. This is not just because of what the enemy might do. There could be another mistaken identity cock-up or the Swordfish may not find *Bismarck*. Time is either dragged out – or compressed so that it flashes by – the worst part being the sitting and waiting. It is inevitable people ponder their mortality and chances of survival. Terry Goddard feels it is better to be a single man with no ties.

> *'I think we knew we were living fairly fast, but I don't think we had any fear of dying. Generally, the guys who bought it were the ones who had just got married or just had a baby. I don't know why. Maybe they took extra time going in to the attack, but they seemed to be the guys who bought it all the time.'*

Motivating himself to keep going was not always easy but on only one occasion did he experience a reluctance.

> *'I believe at one stage, maybe for about a week in the Med, I might have had a twitch, that I was scared of flying, of getting in the cockpit, but despite that I did it.'*

There are no such problems for Goddard now. Refreshed after his sleep, boosted by some bacon sandwiches and a mug of strong tea, he grabs his flying helmet and lifejacket, climbs up through the ship's control island to the Operations Room. It is time for the mission briefing.

> 'We were told where the Bismarck was and where the Sheffield was shadowing. We did have a picture of the Bismarck in Jane's Fighting Ships, so we did know what she looked like. I think we were well aware that Bismarck had to be stopped and we had to stop her. I am not sure that we felt that we were going to sink her but I think when we took off we all had the feeling we certainly were going to damage her and the Home Fleet would be able to engage. We felt okay and happy to be on the strike, but worried about the weather, worried about the ship going up and down. We were amused at seeing the boffins going out – and measuring the rise and fall of the ship and then reporting back to the bridge – and at the dithering as to whether we would or would not fly. We knew perfectly well we were gonna fly, because if we didn't fly there would be no tomorrow for us. We had to fly and weather be darned.'

The aircrews feel the weight of expectation, of history itself – the fate of the Navy and the nation, also the Fleet Air Arm's honour (after the previous day's error) – all pressing down on their shoulders.

The most crucial decision is what kind of detonator pistol the torpedoes should have – contact, which explodes when the torpedo hits the ship, or magnetic, to be detonated by the target vessel's magnetic field.

It is decided contact weapons are best, but this means an hour's delay while magnetic head torpedoes are replaced on each Swordfish. 'It is the sitting around that gnaws at you,' relates Goddard.

> 'You're thinking rather than doing, which is worrisome. Once you start doing things, the worry disappears. It must be tough on God. In war there aren't any atheists – both sides are asking God for help. Most of us say prayers for him to help us. I know I did. Often. Fortunately he was on my side...'

Fifteen Swordfish are ranged on the flight-deck, herring bone fashion, all fuelled up and each armed with a single 18-inch torpedo, ready to go despite the foul conditions.

> 'The ground crews are busy trying to hold the aeroplanes down in this frightful weather.

They are supplemented by volunteers helping to keep them on the flight deck, and they know darned well they are going to be standing out there when the screws are going 'round, which is pretty damned scary. Then you walk to the aeroplane. You had to put on a show … it didn't matter what you felt. You were nonchalant – "it is just a piece of cake". No way anybody is going to know how you felt. You have these magnificent ground crews who are doing an outstanding job. There's no way that they can know that you've got some serious introspective thoughts, and that, just before take-off, you're going to say a prayer.'

7.07 pm – Mr Eden's Reassurance

At the Cabinet War Rooms in London, Foreign Secretary Anthony Eden consoles Churchill with an observation that while 26 May has been a bad day, the *Bismarck* will surely be caught and sunk tomorrow.

7.10 pm – Stormy Take-off

HMS *Ark Royal*

With waves crashing over the carrier's bows, the Swordfish are launched, clawing their way up into the sky. Terry Goddard's aircraft will battle a pitching flight deck washed by the sea.

> 'It's start up – you crank the old thing, get the prop going. One by one, the batsman, the deck control officer, leads you forward – and you just sit and wait, look at the island [the tower] waiting for the green flag and away you go. The ship is steering into wind, actually on this occasion slowed down, so there wasn't too much wind going over the deck. There's green water coming over the bow. In my aircraft – Swordfish 5K – Stan Keane was the pilot; I was the Navigator and Milliner was the Air Gunner. He was responsible for working the radio. I'm responsible for getting us there and Stan is, responsible for flying the aircraft and carrying out the attack. The ship was taking green water. The bow was going up 60ft and down. It was raining, windy, and the ship was rolling and pitching, but there was no problem in take-off: we were airborne before we passed the island.'

Once in the air, the crew of Swordfish 5K formulates a plan of attack – communication within the cockpit is barely possible, what with a 110-knot wind and roar of the aircraft's engine – so they shout to each other down the voice pipe.

> 'We decide what course we're going to steer, what speed we're going to go at, what height we'll go at, whether we'll fly at 5,000 feet or on the deck – actually pretty well everything is done in consultation. When we took off on the strike, we were on our own. The squadron commander, Lt Cdr Tim Coode was nowhere in sight. We did two circuits round the ship, and we picked up two other aircraft and then we set course for Sheffield.'

7.48 pm – Angry Frustration in a U-boat

U-556

Commanded by 25-year-old Kapitänleutnant Herbert Wohlfahrt, this recently commissioned boat experiences a close call with the *Ark Royal* and the *Renown*, which come thundering out of mist from astern of the tiny submarine, almost crushing its periscope in their path but not detecting it.

With no usable weapons remaining, due to being at the end of a patrol, Wohlfahrt is left angry and frustrated. He notes in his War Diary:

> *If only I had a few torpedoes! I would not even*
> *have had to manoeuvre – I was just perfectly*
> *placed for an attack.*

Instead, via the periscope, Wohlfahrt watches Sword-fish 'operating from carrier' – being launched by *Ark Royal* – and reflects on his boat's impotence:

> *I might have been able to help Bismarck.*

The frustration is increased by the fact that *U-556* and her crew have a special bond with the *Bismarck*. Their submarine was also built at Hamburg, on the slipway next to the huge battleship.

When *U-556* was being commissioned in early 1941, the *Bismarck's* band provided the ceremonial music for the event. In return, Wohlfahrt promised to protect the battleship, even issuing a certificate vowing 'before Neptune' that *U-556* would stand by the *Bismarck* 'whatever may befall her…'

Wohlfahrt is already a prodigious sinker of merchant vessels. Since sailing for his latest patrol in *U-556* on 1 May, he has added a trawler and two merchant ships to his tally, which now stands at 21 since October 1939 (nine sunk as captain of *U-14*, six while in command of *U-137*, and now six in *U-556*).

However, using up all the torpedoes so quickly on this sortie ensures *U-556* will only be a spectator when the *Bismarck* most needs help. There are two re-load torpedoes kept externally, under the deck casing of the submarine, but it is not possible to access them due to the rough seas.

Even if it were calm, the likelihood of being spotted by the British on the surface while trying to extract the weapons – and then take them down below via a hatch into the torpedo room – would surely be suicidal, especially with numerous Royal Navy Warships in the locality.

7.50 pm – That Way to Target

Swordfish 5K

The Swordfish turn over the *Sheffield*, this time keeping their torpedoes for the Germans, sailors in the British cruiser pointing the way to *Bismarck*.

Terry Goddard calculates the enemy ship is 12 miles away.

> 'We decided to stay on the deck [low over the sea] and we sighted Sheffield, which obligingly stopped zig-zagging – her counter-U-boat tactic – and she turned towards Bismarck. Sheffield had earlier been terribly sporting in not firing on the idiots attacking them. Sheffield didn't fire at us either – the ship's company were happily waving at us.'

The Swordfish waggle their wings in acknowledgement as they fly past.

> *'Having found Sheffield we decided we would go up through the clag. The Swordfish was the only aircraft that could have flown in those conditions, take-off and landing, indeed going through all that clag as well. We broke at about 5,000ft and we had about 800ft clearance between the two layers of cloud. There was about seven-tenths cloud, so we were getting an occasional glimpse of the sea. At Expected Time of Arrival there was no Bismarck. Now, this was really scary. The threat of disgrace was hanging all over us, so we decided to go back to Sheffield.'*

8.30 pm – Where Is the Enemy?

Swordfish 5K

Terry Goddard is still searching for *Sheffield* in order to get a location check before heading for *Bismarck*.

> *'We went down on the deck right away, which was through the clag. We broke at about 600ft. We found Sheffield and she stopped zig-zagging again and we went up through the cloud again. When we broke from the cloud, we were on our own… So, we went on solo.'*

8.39 pm – Enemy in Sight...

U-556

With his boat on the surface to report in via wireless, Wohlfahrt tells the U-boat force headquarters in Lorient, on the Atlantic coast of occupied France, that he has encountered an enemy 'battleship' and aircraft carrier. This is in fact the battlecruiser *Renown* and the *Ark Royal*. Wohlfahrt conveys their coordinates, hoping this can aid Dönitz in sending out signals from the HQ ordering U-boats to move against the enemy vessels gathering around the *Bismarck*.

8.47 pm – Fire-Spitting Monster

Swordfish Attack

Battling the gale, blown sideways, almost negating their forward momentum, the Swordfish drop from the clouds to make their attack runs.

As they sight oncoming Swordfish, lookouts aboard the *Bismarck* scream: 'Alarm!' The aircraft attack klaxon blares throughout the German battleship.

The *Bismarck* takes violent evasive action, her anti-aircraft guns hurling a storm of steel at the British biplanes. *Bismarck* even fires her main 15-inch guns, the shells sending up tall plumes of spray, hoping to literally knock Swordfish out of the sky. Ken Robinson and other sailors in the *Cossack*, which is loitering at a safe distance having earlier spotted the German battleship, watch the show.

> *'We had sighted the Bismarck and there was another attack of Swordfish. We could see her tracers [shells and bullets] were all different colours going up to the Swordfish — just like fireworks.'*

Among those aviators attracting such a hot reception from the *Bismarck* is Lieutenant Edmund 'Splash' Carver, who is Observer of a Swordfish flown by 818 NAS boss Lt Cdr Tim Coode. Lt Carver has navigated his aircraft safely through the murk and it now dives in to attack.

> *'We came out on Bismarck's port beam … didn't break cloud 'til 700ft and she was steering southeast, making for Brest or something like that. So, of course when we turned in, the wind being in the northwest — with Bismarck going straight downwind — there must've been 30 to 40 knots of wind.*
>
> *'We were tracking across wind during our torpedo run. I think this may have lessened the accuracy of the flak gunners in Bismarck*

because the Swordfish was only doing 90 or 100 knots and was going half as fast sideways as it was forward. I think that must've confused them a bit ... all these billiard balls [anti-aircraft shells] were coming up, flying pretty close. Bismarck, seeing us come in, had managed to turn to port and I don't think we, our [flight's] aircraft got any hits at all. And then we turned away down wind and sat at sea level to observe what went on, and that wasn't easy because of the flak from Bismarck – her [big] guns and anti-aircraft guns – and the spume being blown off the sea ... so we saw her continue manoeuvring for about a quarter of an hour avoiding the other attacks being made after us.

'I couldn't say I saw any hit on her at all. I said to Tim, after about 20 minutes: "I think we ought to say 'No hits, estimate no hits.'"

'He was rather loath to make that signal, and I said: "Well, I think we ought to send it because they want to prepare another lot of aircraft for further attack if only at first light."'

Soon Swordfish 5K will be taking her turn at jousting with the enemy, provided she can find the target. Terry Goddard looks anxiously over the side of the cockpit for some sign of *Bismarck*.

'I had estimated it would be nine minutes to Bismarck, and at just before nine minutes all around us is thundering noise. The whole aircraft shook as if there were a number of express trains roaring by us. We figured Bismarck had opened fire on us. In actual fact she had opened fire on Sheffield, but … we had found her.

'So, down we went. Ice was peeling off the wings, couldn't see a bloody thing. The altimeter is spinning, spinning, spinning and then we break into the clear about 600ft and there's Bismarck on our starboard bow. She was a fire-spitting monster. Everything was coming at us and she was illuminated … awesome. This ship was just magnificent. It looked exactly like a battleship should, I mean scary and everything but just a beautiful ship.

'Once the attack has started, it's all about the pilot. The Observer and the Air Gunner, we just stand by and get really excited watching what is going on. You are not thinking you are going to be killed, you're thinking you're going to hit the bastard and that's it.'

9.05 pm – Torpedo Hit

This is it. The moment of truth for Goddard and Swordfish 5K.

> 'The more you turn [the aircraft] around, and the more you frig around, the more chance they get to hit you, so we just went straight in. We got as low on the deck as we could and went straight. Bismarck was on the port side and she just got bigger and bigger. The flak is bursting over our head. Well above us. The small arms fire is pretty well all around us – and hitting us every once in a while – but we get in to drop the torpedo … do a quick turn away.

> 'Looking back shortly after the turn, I see a large black and white explosion on the Bismarck. It is high and wide. Obviously, it is a torpedo hit. There is no other aircraft anywhere near us and there is no doubt it was the torpedo we had just dropped. I tell Stan, he grunts – he's busy doing various manoeuvres on the deck – I give a message to the Air Gunner that we have scored a hit. Milliner thought he'd seen something too.

> 'Right after the attack the shooting stopped. We were in the clear. She wasn't firing at us. Ark Royal requests us to repeat the message.

Then we climb back up into the clag and this time it is about 6,000ft that we broke clear.

'About five minutes later we saw another Swordfish well ahead. We increase speed, join up with him. It's David Godfrey-Faussett [the other aircraft's pilot] smoking a big cigar and with a smile on his face. I didn't like his course, so we broke away and we headed off on our own.'

9.41 pm – To Any of You That Have Torpedoes

Dönitz issues the order for all available submarines in the Bay of Biscay area that still have torpedoes to converge on *Bismarck*. The Commander U-boats War Log records:

Task: Protection of Bismarck.

This is more in hope than any realistic expectation that submarines will be able to hold off the enemy battle fleet. The atrocious weather will make it hard, if not impossible, to establish and maintain such a shield.

Poor sea-keeping qualities on the surface in a storm mean the tiny U-boats will be forced to crawl along submerged, preserving battery power, which is not only used for propulsion but also to run machinery and lighting.

In heavy seas they cannot surface for long, if at all, to use their diesel engines to make a faster transit and to recharge batteries. That process requires opening hatches to take in air to run the diesels and expel fumes, a wise precaution to also avoid poisoning the crew.

Not only are U-boats an unsuitable type of vessel for the rescue mission, they will likely find it impossible to hit any enemy vessels they do encounter with torpedoes. Calmer seas are needed for torpedoes to be aimed properly and then run true.

The boats that respond anyway are *U-48*, *U-73*, and *U-97*, which will join *U-556* as well as *U-74*. The latter has three torpedoes but is not really combat capable due to sustaining serious depth charge damage when attacked by British warships on 21 May. She is incapable of diving. *U-556* is, of course, toothless. Meanwhile, *U-98* has to decline the mission due to her fuel reserves running too low.

10.06 pm – Grimly Hanging On

U-556

Wohlfahrt persists in his quest to fix the location of British vessels for attack by the other boats if possible:

> *With what remained of my fuel oil I did my best to follow the enemy. Submerged to use*

hydrophones and report results; sent beacon signals.

11.24 pm – Destroyers Attack

HMS *Cossack*

Capt Vian decides he must lead his destroyers in for a torpedo attack despite mountainous seas. If they cannot seriously damage the enemy battleship, they can at least keep the Germans awake all night on edge. This will ensure that when the Home Fleet arrives, the enemy are physically drained and mentally shattered.

11.30 pm – For the Glory of Poland!

ORP *Piorun*

The Polish destroyer ORP *Piorun* had spotted the *Bismarck* around dusk, with the Petty Officer on the range-finder shouting:

'I can see smoke on the horizon!'

Now, the *Piorun* is making so much noise with her screws and so fiercely focussed on attacking *Bismarck*, she charges straight over *U-556* without picking up the enemy submarine on Asdic, the British version of Sound Navigation and Ranging (SONAR).

The equipment is mounted on the bottom of *Piorun*'s hull inside a dome. It can send pulses of sound into the surrounding sea, which, when reflected back from an object, determine range and bearing. The Asdic operator can also listen passively for tell-tale sounds via its hydrophones.

In this instance, the *Piorun*'s high speed means water rushing past the sonar equipment drowns out any possibility of hearing something, such as a U-boat's screws. Had *U-556* still been able to fire torpedoes, this could have been a potentially fatal mistake for the *Piorun*.

With his boat at periscope depth, Kapitänleutnant Wohlfahrt sees a destroyer lunge out of the mist. He later records in his War Diary that, as he ordered *U-556* to go deeper, the enemy vessel 'hurtled over our heads...'

Wohlfahrt is actually more worried about the damage the enemy ship could do to his boat than annoyed at missing a chance to attack. He writes in the War Diary:

> *In the boat we could hear the noise of her propellers. But luck was with us. No depth charges.*

The *Piorun* herself has ten torpedoes, but her captain, Cdr Eugeniusz Plawski, decides he will hold them back while his ship charges in to fire her forward 4.7-inch guns at *Bismarck*.

Tumultuous seas make such a small warship a very unstable gunnery platform, but, nonetheless, Plawski issues the order to open fire to his gunnery officer, adding:

'For the glory of Poland!'

It is not known if any of the *Piorun*'s shells hit the enemy vessel, but it will later be claimed that some were seen flying over the *Bismarck*, but the German ship, in turn, comes close to hitting the Polish warship with 15-inch shells. Somehow, the lucky *Piorun* dodges them, all the while transmitting a defiant wireless signal to the enemy in clear language:

'I am a Pole!'

Petty Officer artificer Pawel Wisniewski, aged 23, admires his captain's reckless courage.

'So, Cdr Plawski [went] straight ahead – [like an] idiot he was going to attack it. We start shelling [using] the 4.7-inch guns. What can you do against a blinking battleship of 50,000 tons? Nothing. They had 15-inch guns!'

Though defiant, Plawski is not an idiot. He knows that his own ship has been so busy with convoy escort duties and other tasks – with barely any torpedo firing practice – it is pointless to fire them until he feels the conditions will give his novices at least a chance of hitting.

Both the *Piorun* and the *Maori* make lunges at *Bismarck* but are silhouetted against the setting sun, making good targets for the battleship's gunners.

As the enemy's 15-inch shells plunge into the sea, Wisniewski ventures out of the destroyer's engine room onto the upper deck for a look at what is happening. Some enemy shells fall very close to the *Piorun*, less than 50 feet away, giving Wisniewski and other Polish sailors a scare or two.

> *'Wheeow! Fountain of water. But he was very*
> *clever was Cdr Plawski…'*

And so, with her captain judging which direction to dodge in order to evade the next shell, the plucky *Piorun* evades destruction. She withdraws while furiously making smoke, in order to try and obscure the aim of the enemy gunners.

HMS *Ark Royal*

The question of torpedo accuracy is of pivotal importance in deciding who will gain the upper hand in the contest, not only in Vian's destroyers but also aboard the British aircraft carrier.

Though the *Bismarck* may have reported torpedo hits to her headquarters at least two hours earlier, for the British, deep doubt still hangs over the result of the strike mission.

With Swordfish landing back aboard the *Ark Royal*, and their crews filing reports, it is decided the balance of probability is that *Bismarck* has not been damaged. This is despite claims in the briefing room by some aviators that they managed torpedo hits on the German giant.

Aircraft, including Terry Goddard's, are still being recovered to the ship, bringing more information – and more claims of hits. 'As usual we orbited for a long time,' Goddard will recall.

> *'We came aboard fairly early so I didn't see the three prangs [crash landings]. Then we went up to briefing. Tim Coode had reported that there were no hits and Command was very reluctant to now accept that there were any. I told them three or four times that we had scored a hit and they ignored me. Finally, when Sheffield sent a report that Bismarck was steering northeast, they suddenly realised that something had happened.'*

In other words, not towards Brest or St Nazaire, but rather back to where the enemy was. Her change in direction could not be happening by choice.

> 'They ultimately accepted that there were two hits. I should point out that when Stan and I attacked the Bismarck, she was steaming northwest rather than the southeast, which we had expected, which in fact meant that we had attacked after the torpedo had hit the rudder. We were the last aircraft to attack the Bismarck, then or any other day.'

'Splash' Carver sees news that the Swordfish have achieved decisive effect greeted with 'joy' and that while one hit had 'rattled the teacups' in *Bismarck*, the other had apparently 'got among her propellers and rudders…' He adds:

> 'We didn't know how long she was going to be unmanoeuvrable of course and [with] the Germans working like beavers to free the rudders…'

11.35 pm – Flag Signals of Hope

HMS *Rodney*

The news of the damage to *Bismarck* has yet to reach other units, and, aboard the *Rodney*, Capt Dalrymple-

Hamilton makes a broadcast from the bridge to his ship's company telling them *Ark Royal*'s attack has failed. His voice dissolves into disappointment, and he clicks the handset off.

Fatigue overcomes him. Dalrymple-Hamilton's eyes are sunken and burned out after days of strain. He leans against the magnetic compass stand on the bridge, tries and fails to light his pipe.

Then a lookout spots new signal flags flying from *King George V* and reports that Admiral Tovey is ordering a course to intercept the enemy.

It appears the valiant aviators have done their bit and succeeded in landing a serious blow after all, but can the *Bismarck* be slowed down even more, or stopped altogether?

KM *Bismarck*

A junior officer reports to Kapitän Lindemann and Admiral Lütjens that the *Bismarck*'s steering appears beyond salvation. Attempts to repair it have so far come to nothing.

Even Gerhard Junack, who is on duty in the battleship's centre turbine room, deep within the citadel, suspects that a fatal blow has been suffered.

Earlier he felt the shock from the torpedo hit on the port rudder through his feet. The deck plates juddered and Junack was provided with further proof when 'water flooded through the port-side gangways into the turbine room, and clouds of gas and smoke filled the room until the forced ventilation cleared it.'

There was flooding in the stern compartments too and men were evacuated from them.

Junack watched as 'the carpenters and repair-crew came through, making their way aft', but the vessel was pitching 'so violently in the strong sea swell that it was impossible to keep a foothold in the turbulent water surging through the companion-way.'

There follows a discussion, at times heated, between Lindemann and the Chief Engineer, Korvettenkapitän Walter Lehman, about how to restore steering control. A hand operated rudder is connected, but this is unworkable, and then an effort to cut away the jammed rudder comes to nothing. A proposal to use explosives to remove it is dismissed, as it risks damage to the propellers.

The bad news is conveyed to the *Bismarck*'s men, with Otto Peters in the battleship's engine room learning that 'we got one hit in our rudder' despite the best efforts to evade enemy torpedoes 'and, when it was hit, it could not be moved anymore.'

The *Bismarck*'s three propellers seem unable to do what might have been possible in other battleships – that is, to steer effectively with the props regardless of the jammed rudders.

It is not possible to keep the ship on a south-easterly course towards the French Atlantic coast, and so, as Junack observes, 'it was therefore necessary to turn head-on to the sea – towards the northwest – at a slow speed, and into the face of the enemy.'

In a situation report to the Kriegsmarine headquarters in Germany, Admiral Lütjens reveals the *Bismarck* is surrounded by enemy forces. She is now unlikely to escape a battle, an injured animal with a British pack of wolves gathering to tear her to shreds.

The *Piorun* and the *Maori* have done their bit, and now the baton has been passed to the *Cossack* and the other destroyers of Capt Vian's 4th Flotilla to make their own attack runs.

11.40 pm – 'We Will Fight'

A signal is sent from the *Bismarck* to German naval headquarters in France by Admiral Lütjens, which states:

> *Ship unable to manoeuvre. We will fight to the last shell. Long live the Führer.*

The Berghof

Hitler receives a telephone call from Grossadmiral Erich Raeder, the commander-in-chief of the

Kriegsmarine, in his operations centre at the main naval headquarters in Berlin.

He tells Hitler the *Bismarck*'s steering has been damaged. The Führer takes this news surprisingly calmly but, on being told that the ship is now unmanoeuvrable, Hitler enquires angrily:

> *'Why is our air force not able to do that sort of thing to the British?'*

An ignoramus on naval matters – loving the prestige that capital ships confer on Germany but having no understanding of naval strategy or tactics – Hitler fails to appreciate the only means to achieve such a feat is via a German aircraft carrier. It is only by deploying aircraft to sea aboard a carrier that the Kriegsmarine could achieve the range and extended time at the scene of battle to send in waves of torpedo-bombers to attack, say, *Ark Royal* or one of the British battleships.

It is doubtful that Raeder dares point out any of this to Hitler on this fraught evening.

11.50 pm – Victory or Death

KM *Bismarck*

With no decisive assistance likely from the Luftwaffe or anyone else, Kapitän Lindemann makes a broadcast to his ship's company, with Otto Peters among those hanging on his every word.

> *'He said: "There's no escape." Because he knew if you cannot steer a ship you can't escape.'*

Lindemann also tells his men they can take whatever they want from the stores. The sailors help themselves to goodies, including tinned ham, cheese in tubes, chocolate, all washed down with brandy, for their last supper. They also take away Swiss watches, aftershave, pocketknives, and even fountain pens. They can have as many cigarettes as they wish.

Reinforcing the men's feeling of their last night on earth, Lütjens makes a mournfully defiant broadcast that he concludes by saying:

> *'For us seamen, the question now is victory or death!'*

Morale collapses; a wave of fear and despair rolls through the ship.

11.58 pm – The Captain Will Not Give Up

Despite the apparent hopelessness of the situation Lindemann decides *Bismarck* must not capitulate entirely to fate, ordering a signal to naval headquarters that her weapons and engines are intact even if the steering is not effective. Perhaps they can hang on until a protective umbrella is thrown over the top by the Luftwaffe's long-range bombers? Maybe U-boats could provide a cordon of safety to deter the British? Might tugs arrive to tow the *Bismarck* to one of the French Atlantic ports?

Such are the straws of hope the desperate men of *Bismarck* grasp.

Admiral Lütjens sends a wireless message to Adolf Hitler, in which he vows:

> *We will fight to the last in our belief of you my Führer, and in the firm faith in Germany's victory.*

11.59 pm – Ship Cannot Be Steered

Lütjens sends another message, again to the naval operational headquarters in France:

> *Armament and engines still intact. Ship however cannot be steered with engines.*

Instructions are signalled by a Kriegsmarine headquarters for the *Bismarck* to send out homing beacon signals to assist U-boats battling heavy seas to reach the scene of battle.

Surfacing his submarine, Wohlfahrt is in a black mood, reflecting:

> *What could I now do to help Bismarck?*

From the bridge of the U-boat, he watches 'star shells and *Bismarck* returning enemy's fire.' And summarises:

> *It's a horrible feeling to be so near and yet not be able to do anything.*

Wohlfahrt decides he will 'keep a lookout and direct those U-boats which still have torpedoes to the scene of the action'.

27 May

Wind – Northwest – force 6–7. Heavy N. W. swell

—Narrative of action between HMS *Rodney* and German Battleship *Bismarck*

00.15 am – Destroyer Attack

U-73

This submarine has already found *Bismarck* – by homing in on the battleship's own beacons. Kapitän-leutnant Helmut Rosenbaum watches through his periscope as Vian's ships go in to attack.

During torpedo runs, the fast and nimble British destroyers change course frequently to avoid being hit by the *Bismarck*'s fire. Combined with the turbulent seas – force 7–9 winds whipping up the surface – this makes it impossible for Rosenbaum in *U-73* to keep his crosshairs on the enemy and successfully launch his own torpedoes.

At his action station on the pom–pom gun – exposed to all the sights, sounds, and dangers of the upper deck – Ken Robinson has a grandstand view. With the scene made gaudy by *Bismarck*'s illumination rounds – fizzing, bright magnesium stars floating down slowly under miniature parachutes – the *Cossack* lunges in.

Ken is waiting for open fire orders from the bridge via his headphones. While the pom–pom is an anti-aircraft weapon – designed to spew out a stream of cannon shells – it has its uses against surface vessels. Ken saw its destructive power off Norway two months earlier, ripping apart enemy fast attack craft during a high-speed raid on a convoy by the 4th Destroyer Flotilla.

> '*We could see the merchant ships and we sank them in no time. We could see the phosphorescent white bow waves of the E-boats – it was a case of just open fire and follow the tracers. The E-boats would vanish really. We never shot any aircraft down, but we sank a few E-boats.*'

Fragile motor-torpedo boats are one thing, but the *Bismarck* is quite another. She is unlikely to feel the sting of *Cossack*'s pom–pom, but they are ready anyway, to contribute if need be. The big guns of the enemy flash and roar, a massive crack like thunder and lightning ripping the night apart. The battleship's smaller calibre weapons twinkle and crackle satanically. As the enemy's heavy shells tear through the sky, they are seen on the *Cossack*'s radar screen, glowing blobs of death tracking across it.

'When the star shells burst, we felt very exposed,' relates Ken Robinson, 'because we'd already had near misses, and it was a bit nervy. And with the ship going everywhere, rather than where it wanted to go. Bismarck was firing the 15-inchers … She didn't hit us but came very close. We tried a few times – going head on into the sea and then turning – and we fired the four torpedoes … We would be straddled with 15-inch shells, then it was up smoke [screen] and out as fast as we could go. The arse-end of the ship was going all over the place with a stern sea. We wanted to get away. We could do 38 knots top speed, but I am sure we were doing more than that and with the sea up our backsides.

'When we did fire our torpedoes, we saw two flashes, and we thought they were hits, but [later] the survivors from the Bismarck said

that, no, we never hit it, and the flashes were
from their guns. We thought we'd hit it. In fact
we were convinced. The only damage that we
suffered was aerials shot away by shrapnel.'

01.53 am – Fury in the Bavarian Alps

The Berghof

The Führer has been kept informed about the recent wireless messages from Lütjens via more telephone calls from Raeder. Now, barely suppressing his fury, he dictates a message for the *Bismarck* to a military aide assigned to his staff. It reads:

> *The whole of Germany is with you. What*
> *can still be done will be done. The performance*
> *of your duty will strengthen our people in the*
> *struggle for their existence. Adolf Hitler.*

A strained silence descends on the Berghof.

Hitler asks how many lives are at risk out there in the Atlantic and is told more than 2,000. The Führer finally erupts in a tirade about the naval top brass who sent the *Bismarck* out without letting him know beforehand.

In the Atlantic, one by one – in attempts at combined attacks – the destroyers run in and out, persevering in dreadful conditions and under heavy fire. Ken Robinson thinks the Poles' performance awesome, but also insane.

> '*Piorun appeared to be working independently, and she was firing 4.7-inch guns or whatever armament she had, going in and firing those. They did daft things like that. They'd fight anybody.*'

Were the rough seas not such a barrier, it is not entirely crazy to think the fighting mad Poles might well ram the *Bismarck*. They seek vengeance for the invasion and brutal occupation of their nation – the Germans even have the audacity to make the Polish port of Gdynia (renamed Gotenhafen) *Bismarck*'s home base. Also, Polish midshipmen were reputedly among those killed when the *Hood* was blown apart.

While not unknown as a tactic when all else fails, ramming is not appropriate for Vian's flotilla, not with the Home Fleet and Force H within striking range.

The best service they can now provide is to maintain contact with the enemy, a duty Innes Hamilton in the *Maori* is keenly aware requires walking a knife edge.

> *'Vian had to do two things – to slow the Bismarck down with torpedo hits, if he could do that, and at the same time make absolutely certain that at least one of his ships was not sunk, so that she could continue to report the Bismarck's position. The Home Fleet of course was lumbering down from the North and would eventually bring her to action … we had the fascinating experience of one Tribal [Class destroyer] at a time going in to attack with torpedoes while the other three lay off and reported the position. We actually hit the Bismarck with a torpedo, and I think at least one of the other Tribals did as well. But such was the construction of the Bismarck – with the best German know-how and fabulous steel – that it made virtually no difference whatever to the Bismarck that we torpedoed her. We all saw a great burst of flame when our [Maori's] torpedo hit the Bismarck, and there were cheers of course from the sailors, but it made no difference whatsoever…'*

It appears to the destroyer men that torpedo hits by the *Maori* and *Cossack* in the early hours cause the *Bismarck* to stop for a short while. In reality, it is just the Germans trying desperately to figure out some means of steering their crippled battleship.

2.36 am – Marked for Destruction

The Home Fleet

Admiral Tovey sends a wireless signal to Capt Vian asking him to identify the *Bismarck*'s position through the remaining hours of darkness:

> *Fire starshell every half hour after all destroyer attacks are completed in order to indicate position of enemy.*

HMS *Cossack*

Though the *Bismarck* continues to fire at Vian's impudent ships whenever she sees an opportunity, for Ken Robinson, and the other destroyer men, it is a case of watching and waiting.

> 'We just hung about then, going in to have a look here and there to see she was not getting any further away because, by this time, she was going in circles. We were waiting for the King George V and Rodney.'

Len Nicholl is sealed inside his twin 6-inch gun turret, trying to snatch a few moments sleep but finding it well-nigh impossible.

> *'We never went to bed that night. We were closed up because Admiral Tovey intended to open fire on Bismarck the next day, so we stayed at our Action Stations right through. It was quite tiring really to be sat 'round a gun ail night, and you couldn't sleep, or at least get what you'd call sleep. It was too blinkin' cold anyway in the turret. There's no heating, nothing like that. We were sat there from about eight o'clock that evening.'*

At one stage it appears the *Rodney* might have to do the job on her own, and this does not amuse Nicholl and his shipmates.

> *'The King George V was going to pull away anyway from the fight before we met the Bismarck because she was running out of oil. The Rodney had been at sea for over a week, [but] we still had stacks of oil aboard... It really got up the nose of most of Rodney's crew. Tovey was saying to us that he may have*

to leave us to it, which wasn't a very good thought.'

2.51 am – Heartiest Congratulations

KM *Bismarck*

Despite messages broadcast throughout the ship telling them attempts are being made to send out aircraft and U-boats to save them, despair in the *Bismarck*'s old salts deepens. Hope stills glows in the hearts of inexperienced sailors, but the veterans know their commanders are just trying to maintain morale in the face of hopeless odds.

3.00 am – Vital to Course of the War

HMS *King George V*

Determining there is in fact enough fuel remaining to fight the *Bismarck* and also get home, a message from Admiral Tovey is pinned up on notice boards throughout the ship. It is a call to action for the approaching battle. Tovey tells the flagship's sailors and marines:

> *The sinking of Bismarck may have an effect on the war as a whole out of all proportion to the loss of one battleship. May God be with you and grant victory.*

A staff officer at the Luftwaffe headquarters rings the Berghof to let the Führer know that aircraft have taken off to try and find the *Bismarck* now that she is closer to France. If possible, they will attack the British warships, but the distance is at extreme range and there can be no guarantee of success.

Hitler goes to bed with faint hope kindled that Germany's humiliation can be avoided but nurturing the bitter notion that it would have been better to lose the *Bismarck* trying to finish off *Prince of Wales* on 24 May.

3.51 am – Tribute for Sinking the *Hood*

A signal is received from Admiral Raeder revealing the Führer has confirmed the award of the Knight's Cross to the *Bismarck*'s gunnery officer, Lieutenant Commander Adalbert Schneider, for sinking *Hood*. The signal tells Schneider:

Heartiest congratulations.

3.52 am – Still Hanging On

U-556

Wohlfahrt has decided his submarine will head south, 'in order to keep abeam of the running fight.' The boat's fuel situation is becoming critical, however, and Wohlfahrt notes that he 'shall soon have to break off…'

In the rough sea conditions, the submarine's oil fuel has become 'all but exhausted' and what is left is required for a fast surface transit to reach the U-boat's home base in France.

U-556 will for now be compelled to dive and use electric propulsion, meaning she crawls along, relying on hydrophones to pick up sounds of combat and try to assess what is happening from a distance. In the prevailing sea conditions, which create a lot of background noise in the sea, the battle will soon pass beyond effective hydrophone range.

4th Destroyer Flotilla

Vian's destroyers fire star shells to indicate the location of the *Bismarck* to the Home Fleet commander, as he prepares to launch his forces at the crippled and harassed enemy.

6.30 am – Rendezvous in Fierce Seas

U-556

Surfacing to send a last radio report to HQ, *U-556* makes a rendezvous with *U-74*, commanded by Kapitänleutnant Eitel-Friedrich Kentrat, to pass over 'the task of maintaining contact', with the two captains shouting to each other via megaphones as their boats ride fierce seas.

6.50 am – Holding Back

ORP *Piorun*

As light streaks the horizon and the weather clears, Cdr Plawski's *Piorun* again sights *Bismarck*, though the German battleship is from time to time obscured by rain squalls and slipping in and out of fog. Earlier, at 5.00 am, Plawski was told by Capt Vian to head back to Plymouth and refuel, but the Pole is still itching to use his torpedoes. Plawski tells his crew over the public address system:

> '*We are going to make a torpedo attack.*'

However, the *Maori* lies between the *Piorun* and the *Bismarck*, and so Petty Officer Pawel Wisniewski and his shipmates learn, to their great disappointment, that 'we couldn't fire torpedoes or you would hit him [the *Maori*].'

6.55 am – Close with the Enemy

HMS *Rodney*

On his bridge, Captain Dalrymple-Hamilton reads a light signal message from Tovey advising him that, come dawn, the boss intends *King George V* and *Rodney* to close with the enemy.

Half an hour earlier, Force H commander Vice Admiral Somerville risked a wireless signal to advise Tovey of a new Swordfish attack:

Striking Force expected to arrive at 0715.

It seems the *Bismarck* will be assailed from above, too, but, in the meantime, the destroyers have time enough to get in more attacks.

HMS *Maori*

The warship now finds herself in a quite amazing predicament in an episode that perfectly illustrates the defiant courage of the destroyer men and the kind of informal – and sometimes testy – relationship that can exist between a captain and his subordinate officers.

Come the dawn, Innes Hamilton is at his action station on the *Maori*'s bridge alongside Cdr Harold 'Beaky' Armstrong.

> *'In the morning, while it was very foggy, and the other three Tribals had lost touch, the Bismarck emerged out of a fog bank, and the Maori was the only ship left in contact. When you realise that the Maori was one destroyer and the Bismarck was the most powerful ship*

> *that, perhaps, the world has ever seen — and*
> *the distance between us was about 3,000 yards*
> *— it was certainly a moment in the lives of*
> *everybody present.'*

Cdr Armstrong turns to Lt Hamilton and remarks:

> *'Number One, I think we will finish the*
> *Bismarck off ourselves.'*

This statement is made with brilliant, British under-stated good humour – laced with knowledge that the finest traditions of the Royal Navy require such a feat. His second in command has a different perspective on what is needed.

> *'Sir, if I may say so, that would be a*
> *grave mistake. It is absolutely essential that*
> *Churchill can announce that our Home Fleet*
> *have caught up with the Bismarck — and the*
> *British fleet has sunk her — and that is the end*
> *of the saga. For you to sink the Bismarck casu-*
> *ally out of hand, by torpedo from one destroyer,*
> *would be an anti-climax of a terrible nature.'*

Cdr Armstrong gives his second-in-command a robust response, making it clear who is boss and what *must* happen.

'Number One, I will have no more comments like that from you, and, if I do, I will put you in irons, so help me.'

Hamilton realises the captain is not to be diverted from his admirable, if possibly suicidal, intent.

'This was on the bridge of a destroyer in the middle of the Atlantic with the world's greatest warship 3,000 yards away in a fog bank. It was a moment I will never forget. 'Beaky' Armstrong said: "I will stop the ship and turn very slowly and the Gunner T [the Warrant Officer in charge of the weapons] will fire the torpedoes himself."

'He put on five degrees of rudder and stopped the ship's engines to make absolutely certain that we hit the Bismarck with the torpedoes. As the first torpedo slid into the water, the Bismarck opened fire with all her armament... One 15-inch shell went under our wireless aerials. Splinters hit the ship, the captain went full ahead, and we made smoke, dropped smoke floats … and everything else. We zig-zagged, and we got away, and the Bismarck did not hit us.'

6.59 am – Honour Satisfied

ORP *Piorun*

As the *Maori* finally clears out of the way, the *Piorun* makes her torpedo run at top speed, the *Bismarck* firing both the 15-inch and secondary armament, creating massive shell plumes all around the little destroyer.

Shrapnel rains down on the *Piorun*'s upper deck and superstructure, but no hits are suffered. It still makes life difficult for the *Piorun*, which finds the view of target obscured by the masses of collapsing spray.

Opening fire with her forward four 4.7-inch guns, the *Piorun* then turns beam on to the *Bismarck*, making smoke to try and hide while preparing to launch torpedoes. But there is still no clear chance of hitting, so Plawski finally concedes it is time to depart the field of battle, but with Polish honour well satisfied. Besides, the lack of fuel compels him to do so.

The *Piorun* fends off three attacks by enemy aircraft on the way to Plymouth, using the last reserves of fuel for evasive manoeuvres.

7.00 am – *Bismarck*'s Final Message Home

For the German naval high command, confirmation that virtually all hope is lost comes when Admiral Lütjens signals that he wants his War Log collected by a U-boat. With *U-556* having gone, *U-74* picks up this task. It will not be easy in such rough weather or in sight of numerous enemy units – especially for a boat that is not currently capable of submerging. The task will potentially require the submarine to expose herself to attack.

7.07 am – Beware U-boats

Aware of enemy submarine activity from intelligence sources in occupied Europe – and via its ability to detect the origins and destinations of enemy signals traffic – the Admiralty sends a warning to Admiral Tovey in *King George V*. It suggests that while one U-boat could have generated all the signals, it is likely to be more:

> *Best guess is that 4 U-boats made signals.*

At the same time Admiral Somerville, of Force H, lets Tovey know he will not, after all, be joined by Swordfish for the final assault:

> *Have cancelled attack due to difficulties in identification of own ships in low visibility.*

7.08 am – Are You Ready?

HMS *King George V*

Via a light signal Tovey flashes his concise tactical instructions and intentions to Capt Dalrymple-Hamilton:

> *Am changing course to look for enemy. Keep station 1200 yards or more as you desire and adjust your bearings. If I do not like the first set-up I may break off the engagement at once. Are you ready to engage?*

Rodney acknowledges.

7.25 am – If Opportunity Permits

HMS *King George V*

As a former CO of *Rodney* in the mid-1930s, Tovey is well aware that, unlike his newer flagship, the older vessel has torpedo tubes mounted in her bows, below the waterline. He flashes Dalrymple-Hamilton:

> *If opportunity permits fire your torpedoes.*

HMS *Rodney*

Midshipman Yves Dias is at his action station on *Rodney's* bridge near the Captain. He sees *King George*

V's signal lamp flashing the message. It means a special responsibility, for, as Second Torpedo Officer, it will be his job to lay those weapons on target.

> '*I had these huge binoculars, which you couldn't hold – they were on a stand, which I manoeuvred and so transmitted information down to the torpedo control centre.*'

Provided with that data, the Torpedo Officer, Lt Cdr Roger Lewis, will give orders to fire torpedoes as and when he feels Tovey's desired opportunity arises. Yet, amid the grim spectacle of battle unfolding before his eyes, Yves will not even notice the torpedoes launching.

7.30 am – The Cold Light of Day

High up on top of *Rodney*'s massive command tower, in the very thinly armoured Air Defence Position (ADP), Lieutenant Donald Campbell scans the surrounding sea with his binoculars. He considers the looming battle 'a cold uninviting prospect to weary men already shocked by loss of *Hood* and three days and nights of alarms, excitement and disappointment.'

7.45 am – Today My Wife Will Become a Widow

KM *Bismarck*

The German battleship's fourth gunnery officer, Lieutenant Burkard von Müllenheim-Rechberg decides to take one last tour of his beloved battleship. He finds many men below decks and on the upper deck lying down asleep at their guns and other action stations. It is as if they are already dead. In the ship's wardroom he finds officers in a dark mood. One of them remarks:

> *'Today my wife will become a widow, but she doesn't know it.'*

7.50 am – Songs and Cheers

HMS *Rodney*

In the X-turret of the *Rodney*, the rough hands of Royal Marine gunners apply grease to the breeches of the big 16-inch guns.

Through voice-pipes linking the huge turret to the shell handling rooms and magazines below singing and cheering can be heard as men celebrate the coming battle. This is their chance to avenge the *Hood*, to defeat a vessel of war created by a genocidal fascist regime, and to avenge the 1941 firebombing of their homes in Plymouth, Portsmouth, on the Mersey, and elsewhere.

The fate of the *Hood* is something the men of the *Rodney* have both pondered privately and discussed several times over the past few days. For all their fears – mainly kept private – there is clearly no feeling of going to their doom. Len Nicholl acknowledges that may have been due to ignorance about their own ship's vulnerabilities.

> '*I heard afterwards that Rodney was quite susceptible to the same problem as Hood, where she didn't have an armoured bulkhead up for'ard between the ammunition magazines. If Rodney was, say, heading straight towards an enemy ship and they fired and hit her up for'ard it could have caused the same damage as the Hood, but we didn't know it at the time. We were always informed that Rodney was so well armoured. The front of the 16-inch turrets was 32-inches thick and that is some thickness. Rodney had an armoured deck from stem to stern – in places it was 12 inches thick – but where that bomb penetrated the ship off Norway it was only four inches despite protecting the 6-inch and 4.7-inch magazines. The 16-inch ammunition*

magazines were protected by about 12 inches of armour, but we never thought Rodney would be in the same position as the Hood … it was a pretty daunting thing to face Bismarck.'

With hours confined in his cold, clammy 6-inch gun turret and unable to sleep, Nicholl mulls over the arbitrary nature of war – how one set of sailors or marines can be drafted to one ship and be killed while others, sent to another vessel, live. He has been lucky to serve in *Rodney*, at least so far. His mind drifts back to the men of the *Hood*, some of whom he'd met ashore.

'I was sat in Scapa Flow canteen with a Petty Officer from Hood. The PO from Hood said he had always wished there was more eleva-tion on the guns on his ship – more like the elevation of the 16-inch guns of the Rodney. I always understood that if you had more eleva-tion on a gun you could stand off a bit farther out. Speaking to a gunnery officer that was on the Rodney after the war he said: "No. Elevation doesn't make any difference to the range of a gun – the higher the guns are the less range there is on the shell."

'That PO who talked to me about the guns went down with the Hood. He obviously had

some doubt about the firepower of his vessel.
Pity really because she was such a massive ship.
Rodney sailed with her a couple of times in
the North Sea in the early part of the war.
One time I spotted a broom handle in the
water and somebody thought it was a periscope.
The whole fleet dispersed at different angles. I
watched the Hood pull away at full speed and
it was terrific to watch. She certainly left us far
behind that particular morning. I never ever
doubted the fact that she was a brilliant ship,
but to lose her like that was a helluva blow.
The Hood still gets into peoples' minds. We
should never have lost her really.'

For most of a capital ship's crew, death can come
without them seeing it approaching. They will hear
the rumble of battle beyond the armoured hull, feel
the great vibration of their own ship's engines and
weapons firing, but otherwise they are blind. The vast
majority of the men are buttoned up below decks. As
the aimer for a 6-inch gun turret Nicholl is one of
those who can see everything with shocking clarity.

'There was very few able to see what was going
in, even in our turret. The turret trainer and
the Corporal was sat beside the turret aimer.
The Corporal had the same monocular as I

had. *We could see what was happening, but the rest of turret couldn't as they were closed up around the gun. There's no way they can look out. I think the turret had a little bit of a periscope, which the captain of the turret could use. Even the crews of the 16-inch guns couldn't see anything because they were completely enclosed in the gun-house. With the 6-inch turrets they had these two sighting ports with covers to keep the sea out if you are not using the turret – that is, if it is trained fore and aft, and you are running in rough weather. Without those sighting port covers you'd have all the water going in the turrets or in the gun-houses. They take them down during firing. It is just a case of undoing a couple of cleats. I was right beside one of these sighting ports and could see everything.'*

7.55 am – No Words Left

KM *Bismarck*

Lt von Müllenheim-Rechberg enters the *Bismarck*'s bridge, spotting Kapitän Lindemann eating breakfast – some black bread, cheese and ham, washed down with coffee.

As he munches, the Captain stares blankly out of the bridge windows. Von Müllenheim-Rechberg stands next to him, expecting some words of encouragement. Lindemann says nothing.

7.57 am – End of the Ordeal... Or Just the Beginning?

HMS *Rodney*

In the main gunnery control post, just under the ADP at the top of the battleship's command tower, 25-year-old Leading Seaman Tommy Byers, from Northern Ireland, remarks to another sailor that perhaps their ordeal is about to end. The other man observes sourly that perhaps it has only just begun. From his seat on a platform above them, the Gunnery Officer, Lieutenant Commander William Crawford, tells the older rating to cut it out.

Having joined the Royal Navy in the early 1920s, Crawford served as a midshipman in the battleship *Barham*. By the middle of that decade, 34-year-old Crawford had specialised as a gunner after sea time in the destroyer *Vansittart* and the battleships *Warspite* and *Revenge*. Seeing service in the *Queen Elizabeth* and the carriers *Ark Royal* and *Furious*, Crawford was then appointed to the cruiser *Delhi*, which undertook so-called 'Non-Intervention Patrols' during the Spanish Civil War of the late 1930s. The aim was to protect merchant shipping, try to stop arms smuggling, and generally prevent the conflict from spreading to the rest of Europe. While the *Delhi* was in port at Palma, Mallorca, Crawford met several Kriegsmarine officers and thought them 'quite friendly ... they were pretending to be benevolent neutrals, like us.'

Yet the Germans had just reoccupied the Ruhr (in March 1936) and, like the Italians and Russians, would intervene militarily in the civil war. Crawford felt, 'it was beginning to appear that they [the Germans] were going to be pretty belligerent in Europe.'

Following the Munich Crisis of September 1938, after which British Prime Minister Neville Chamberlain promised 'peace for our time', Crawford recognised that war with the Nazis would soon come.

He believed the Royal Navy was 'on the whole well prepared ... the ships that were in commission were in a good state' with 'battle skills' well-rehearsed. The *Rodney*, which he joined in early July 1940, was 'a wonderful ship, very, very happy ... and I think a very efficient ship...' But he remembers that wasn't always the case:

> *'They were very, very difficult times...[the Rodney was] a Devonport manned ship and [the blitz of Plymouth in 1941 meant] it was a terribly anxious time for a very large number of our ship's company who possibly got no news of their families...'*

Now Crawford found German belligerence manifested in the *Bismarck* filling his optics. Knowing he would soon have to engage in combat, he thinks about the outcome:

> 'Our chances were very good. Pretty confident in our own gunnery. We knew we had some disadvantages and advantages.'

7.59 am – Ghost Ship

KM *Bismarck*

Von Müllenheim-Rechberg passes through the charthouse, on his way back to his own action station in the gunnery control position for the two aft 15-inch gun turrets. The compartment appears deserted, and he pauses to look at the chart, which is illuminated by a single lamp. With a finger, von Müllenheim-Rechberg traces the *Bismarck*'s route from her battle with *Hood* in the Denmark Strait. In his head, he hears the cheers of triumph from a few days earlier, remembers someone shouting: 'She has blown up, we have destroyed the *Hood*!'

His finger follows the *Bismarck*'s course all the way down to where she was hit in her steering by the Swordfish torpedo.

Looking around, von Müllenheim-Rechberg spots some dark shapes in the shadows on the deck, gradually making out two sailors lying down, awaiting their fate.

Spooked by this, he decides to make his exit. As he leaves, someone shouts down the voice pipe from the bridge:

'Enemy in sight.'

Back in his gunnery control position, von Müllenheim-Rechberg presses his eyes against the cups of his targeting optics. Adjusting magnification and focus, he is greeted with the chilling sight of two 'bulky silhouettes, unmistakably the *King George V* and *Rodney*.'

The enemy are coming on relentlessly, seeming to exude the dark determination of remorseless executioners. Every muscle in his body tightening with anticipation, von Müllenheim-Rechberg feels the men of *Bismarck* will do their duty. Combat will provide a release from the torment of this dark night of the soul. After all, he reflects, 'we could be shot to pieces only once.'

8.00 am – Some Huge Thing

HMS *Rodney*

In the Air Defence Position, Lt Campbell twiddles the focus knob on his optics. A rain squall moment-arily obscures a shape on the horizon, around 14 miles' distance. It is swept aside, revealing the target: *Bismarck*.

On the *Rodney*'s bridge, the Gunnery Officer's simultaneous sighting report is overheard by Yves Dias, who reflects:

> '*It's got to be some huge thing that's seen at that distance.*'

The forthcoming battle will involve 5,000 British sailors and marines pitted against 2,365 Germans, the brutal, bloody conclusion to a chase stretching across 1,750 miles and lasting five days. It will be seared into the memory of Len Nicholl.

> '*To me it was quite a day. You will never forget the date, the 27th. Never.*'

8.15 am – *Norfolk*'s Close Calls

HMS *Norfolk*

Of all the warships engaged in the assault on the *Bismarck*, it is the heavy cruiser *Norfolk* that has dogged her the longest and now has yet another rather too close encounter with the enemy.

With the *Suffolk*, she had shadowed the enemy from the evening of 23 May and at one point dodged a sorely aggravated *Bismarck*'s heavy shells.

After the German ship pulled off her temporary disappearing act, the *Norfolk* participated in the search for *Bismarck*, which looked pretty futile at one stage. Young Lieutenant of Royal Marines John Ruffer recorded in his diary notes on the afternoon of 25 May:

> *Dimmed hope.*

Ruffer was very happy to report on 26 May that contact was regained.

> *Catalina sighted her. Lost touch. Ark Royal confirmed.*

And then, after fearing it was 'too long a stern chase', Ruffer recorded on the evening of 26 May:

> *2 hits – 1 probable.*

On the morning of 27 May, in his action station within the *Norfolk*'s gunnery director position, Ruffer stares out at a 'bleak dawn, with a flicker of a watery sun to come, low down through the driving clouds.' His job in any battle will be to use high powered optical instruments to target the enemy.

As *Norfolk* ploughs on, Ruffer scrutinises the narrow silhouette of a mystery ship eight miles in

the distance, struggling to make an exact identific-
ation amid a gale with the sea whipped up. With the
distance shortening, it turns out to be the *Bismarck*,
with *Norfolk*'s gunnery officer crying out:

'*There she is!*'

Ordered to ensure the cruiser's 8-inch guns are properly laid on the enemy and standing by to fire, Ruffer
responds:

'*All guns ready.*'

The *Norfolk* hurtles towards *Bismarck* at 20 knots,
rather than keeping a wise and respectful distance.
While the gunnery control team realise it is the
German monster ship looming ever larger, those on
the bridge did not seem to get the message from the
gunnery officer that *Bismarck* is ahead. There, the
Bismarck is being mistaken for *Rodney*, and a telegraphist on the bridge wing is asked to flash her a
friendly light signal.

At last the message from the gunnery director
confirming it is *Bismarck* reaches the very tired captain
and his officers of the watch. Capt Alfred Philips
orders the *Norfolk*'s wheel hard over, and the cruiser
makes off in the opposite direction. The *Bismarck* does
not even bother to fire at the cruiser. The British

battleships cannot be ignored. Over the next half hour or so, those in action stations on the Bismarck can observe the enemy's approach and do so with a deep sense of foreboding.

8.47 am – Shoot!

HMS *Rodney*

Having taken their time getting into the right position and closing the range, the British battleships can begin their grim work. Aboard the *Rodney*, Lt Cdr Crawford receives a drily humorous message from the captain.

> '...*we'd been closed up in our action stations all night. And as the dawn broke – a pretty murky dawn – I sighted the Bismarck on the horizon. I reported to the bridge that the Bismarck was in sight. I believe my captain was dozing in his chair at the time. And the navigator gave him a nudge and said: "Gunnery Officer says Bismarck in sight, Sir." And the captain's reaction – he was a very trusting man – was: "Why hasn't he opened fire?" Normally, of course, the routine is, before you go into action, if you sight a ship, you have to get the captain's permission to open fire.*'

Crawford obliges Captain Dalrymple-Hamilton without further delay despite less than ideal circumstances.

> *'Conditions for the rangefinders were very bad. We were steaming at full speed. There was a lot of vibration. There was a tremendous lot of spray. And the only ranges that I got from my rangefinders were obviously incorrect. And, working from my knowledge of the distance of the horizon from the position where I was in the control tower, in fact I opened fire entirely on a guessed range…'*

There is a loud ting-ting of bells within the *Rodney* warning that the main armament is about to fire. A single 16-inch shell is hurled at the *Bismarck* to test accuracy, the range around 13 miles. It splashes wide of target, and then, with calculations adjusted, there is a deafening crash as the six 16-inch guns of A and B turret send their shells towards *Bismarck*.

Sixty seconds later the *King George V* fires a salvo with her 14-inch guns, sounding to Lt Campbell in *Rodney* like a 'dull drum-beat'.

The British shells miss their mark, creating gigantic shell splashes around the *Bismarck* but causing no harm.

8.49 am – Target *Rodney*

KM *Bismarck*

Deciding to concentrate on knocking out the most dangerous of her opponents – HMS *Rodney* – guns flash and the German battleship's silhouette is enveloped in huge clouds of smoke.

HMS *King George V*

As the shells plunge in, a young officer observing from a gunnery control position in the Home Fleet Flagship watches the sea around the *Rodney* erupt. He thinks she has been hit and must surely go the way of the *Hood*.

Instead of *Rodney* exploding, the long, ugly silhouette of the battleship emerges from amid the collapsing, shrapnel-laced geysers. The huge blocky bridge superstructure gives the impression of a knight's helmet as he crouches low down in the saddle of his steed in a joust.

HMS *Tartar*

Sub Lieutenant Ludovic Kennedy, aged 21, watches from the wings aboard the *Tartar* – which, like all the destroyers, is not required to take part as the drama of the big ships commences.

The *Tartar*, along with the HMS *Mashona* and HMS *Somali* had been ordered to accompany the *Rodney* when she departed from escorting the troop ship *Britannic* across the Atlantic to go and hunt the *Bismarck*.

The navy is in Sub Lt Kennedy's blood – his father was a career RN officer, and so Ludovic volunteered straight out of Oxford University and began training in 1940.

Meanwhile, his father, Captain Edward Kennedy, was too old to be given a warship command and was instead made the CO of the Armed Merchant Cruiser HMS *Rawalpindi*.

Conducting a patrol to the south of Iceland in late November 1939, the *Rawalpindi* had the misfortune of crossing paths with the *Gneisenau* and *Scharnhorst* to the south of Iceland. While they had nine 11-inch guns each, the smaller and slower *Rawalpindi* had only eight 6-inch guns.

'I think, everybody in the *Rawalpindi* probably knew their number was up,' Ludovic Kennedy would reflect some years later on the fate of his father's ship.

> '...there was a brief battle, just as it was getting dark. My father's ship got one hit on the quarter deck of the Gneisenau [actually the Scharnhorst], but it was a one-sided battle

> *— it took about 15 minutes. The Rawalpindi*
> *was set ablaze and my father and most of his*
> *ship's company and all his officers were killed*
> *or drowned.'*

The sacrifice made by Capt Kennedy and 237 of his men deterred the raiders from carrying on with their attempt to break out into the Atlantic. The German battlecruisers realised *Rawalpindi* had sent a message to say she had spotted them and that every Royal Navy warship available would be sent to destroy them. So they turned around, soon heading home to Germany.

Eighteen months after his father's heroism, Ludovic Kennedy finds himself involved in an attempt to sink the most powerful surface raider Hitler has at his disposal.

—

The *Tartar's* captain, Commander Lionel Skipworth, now receives a signal from Admiral Tovey advising him to:

> *Proceed in execution of previous orders when*
> *convenient.*

Kennedy recalls that 'previous orders were to return to oil at Londonderry'…

'...I remember the Captain saying: "Well, as 'convenient' is up to me, I think we'll stick around for a bit and watch the battle." ... suddenly we saw the Bismarck — it was this huge, great black bulk, of vast, sinister appearance ... the enemy come out of its lair and prowling about the Atlantic. And the Rodney and the King George V both opened fire, and the thing I think most of us remember at that time were the colour contrasts ... the brown of the cordite from the guns [firing], the green of the sea with little white caps, the blue bits of sky ... and the blackness of the Bismarck and the greyness of the British ships. We just sat back and watched.'

8.51 am – Straddled

HMS *Rodney*

Yves Dias is impressed by the *Bismarck*'s shooting, finding it 'extraordinary – one shot over, one shot under.' Through his glasses, the *Bismarck* is frighteningly close.

'It looked as if it was next door to you, it was so huge. In fact you could see Bismarck's shells coming towards you and you could see our

shells going away from us. It really was a bit of a shocker. King George V kept well astern of us, probably a couple of miles or so and more or less left us to do the job. I was scared, certainly. You'd be a fool not to be … but you got on with the job. You kept going. You weren't frightened for the whole time because you were so young anyway. You didn't realise that you could be blown away at any minute.'

The Germans have a fearsome reputation for accuracy. It was first established during the Battle of Jutland in May 1916 where they blew apart three British battlecruisers, and damaged several battleships, due to incredibly well aimed heavy shells. The demise of the *Hood* seems to reinforce that reputation in the minds of their foes, including Len Nicholl. He watches from his turret as the flames and smoke of guns firing ripple along the entire length of *Bismarck*. He counts down the seconds to potential hits on the *Rodney*, while remaining confident his own ship's 16-inch guns will be on target.

'You can take nothing away from the Germans, their gunnery was out of this world, really. Even the most ardent British sailor would give way to the fact that the Germans were better at naval gunnery than we were,

though at the time the Rodney met her, we were in our prime as far as our training was concerned and our skill at gunnery…'

That the *Bismarck* has failed so far to score a hit on the *Rodney* is also down to Captain Dalrymple-Hamilton, whom Yves Dias watches coolly steering the ship out of harm's way.

'Due to very clever manoeuvring, he avoided shells. He was a very calm man. Nothing seemed to worry him at all. He conned the ship beautifully. He'd get a salvo landing all around and he would just shift his ship, almost as if he knew where the next shot was coming. He was very astute. You had every confidence in him.'

While Dalrymple-Hamilton's masterly control of his battleship is crucial, there is no doubt that the *Bismarck* herself is not on top of her game.

Yet, while *Bismarck* continually misses her target, her High Explosive (HE) shells are exploding upon hitting the water, with shrapnel puncturing the *Rodney*.

Inside the ADP, Lt Campbell and his team flinch as a large piece cuts through its thin skin, like a hot knife through butter. It harms nobody – until a sailor picks it up, yelling with pain as it burns his hand. Shrapnel slices into the massive, towering Octopoidal – the ship's massive octagonal bridge structure – creating at least one ragged hole. Parts of the hull are also peppered.

9.00 am – More Hits Needed

HMS *King George V*

The *Bismarck* now fires on the Home Fleet flagship. On the Admiral's Bridge, the Fleet Gunnery Officer loudly announces his estimate of how long it will take the enemy shells to reach *King George V*.

> *'Time of flight fifty-five seconds!'*

He begins the count down to the moment of possible impact.

Admiral Tovey tells him off:

> *'It is better not to know the exact moment when a 15-inch shell hits us in the stomach.'*

In the *King George V*'s Gunnery Director position an officer exclaims:

> *'Our High Explosive shells are bouncing off – switch to armour piercing!'*

Meanwhile, Tovey picks up a phone to tell the battle-ship's CO, Captain Wilfred Patterson:

> *'Close the range! Get closer! I can't see enough hits.'*

If having someone deliver a countdown to a potential shell impact is too much to bear for an admiral who *can* see what is going on, imagine what it is like for the vast majority of people in the *King George V*.

Like those aboard HMS *Rodney*, the flagship's men cannot see a thing. Locked up in compartments and other spaces deep inside the ship they must hold their nerve, as bangs, crashes, and thumps – which may or may not be enemy shells ripping into their vessel – reverberate all around them.

They must do their jobs as human cogs in the complex machinery of a battleship in combat. Among them is Peter Bridewell, a young Royal Marine working in a cordite chamber below one of *King George V*'s 5.25-inch secondary twin gun turrets.

> *'We had been told that we were not going to attack until the morning, and so to get as much rest as we could. Breakfast would be served at five o'clock and we'd have Action Stations and then we'd attack. It duly worked out that way.'*

Over the ship's public address system, an officer in a position to see the outside world provides a running commentary on what is happening for those closed up below decks, He tells them:

'We're now going into the attack – stand by.'

While he and the other members of the 5.25-inch gun turret crew wait for the range to shorten, Bridewell is able to pick up the sound of the 14-inch guns opening fire, hearing 'quite a crashing sound.' This is followed by 'another crashing sound'…

'…and then an almighty crash … and I thought to myself: "Well, that's either something hit us, or we've changed to a broadsides." Which in fact we had … the 14-inch guns were straddling Bismarck. I said to my mate: "We've straddled Bismarck" … We had a report come through: "Bismarck is firing back, but their shells are falling short." We knew that German ships were supposed to hit with their first shell. They weren't doing it this time, but if they were falling short, it was pretty sure the next one would be accurate. After a little while, Bismarck was still firing back, but they were still short. I said: "Well that tells me one thing – our guns are longer range than Bismarck's, *and Bismarck are doing their best, but they can't touch us.'"*

In fact, the *Bismarck* has already suffered dreadful damage. Her ability to hit back is severely degraded, due to the ship's command and control positions, and the people in them, likely having been eviscerated by multiple shell hits.

9.02 am – A Long Dash to Battle

HMS *Dorsetshire*

After her long dash from the south, the heavy cruiser *Dorsetshire* storms into the fight.

It is the culmination of a struggle to maintain speed across many miles in heavy seas, with engines at full pelt, the ship trembling and shuddering as she dug her bows in, then sprang free from long, rolling swells. At one point during the race to battle *Dorsetshire* plunged past a merchant vessel, gun turrets turning as if sniffing out prey. A quick exchange of urgent signal lamp messages ascertained the steamer's friendly identity – and then the guns trained away again as the cruiser battered her way north, disappearing into the murk, intent on her mission to intercept the *Bismarck*. She left in her wake merchant mariners grateful not to have been blasted by mistake in the foul conditions.

Now the *Dorsetshire* is finally at the scene of battle, and with the weather beginning to clear a little. Standing on the cruiser's bridge beside Capt Martin, teenage rating George Bell takes in the amazing scene.

> '*Bismarck was getting a really good pounding and she was already slowed down, we found later that was because her steering gear had been damaged ... I think we began to realise then that it was only a question of time but hoping also that we weren't going to end up with any damage.*'

Swinging broadside on to target, the *Dorsetshire* fires all her 8-inch guns. Capt Martin, on an exposed bridge wing, is doused in sea spray. He turns to a rating beside him to grab a fresh pair of binoculars so he can see whether or not shells are hitting *Bismarck*.

As if in reply, a young officer's voice screams over the speaker system:

> '*Got her that time!*'

Shell splashes surround *Bismarck*. She shudders with hits from shells of the British battleship big guns as well as secondary weapons. The latter are almost as big in calibre as the main guns of the British cruisers. Watching from the *Rodney*, Yves Dias finds it a terrible sight.

> '*We noted that our shells, which were one ton in weight and the biggest in the world at sea, were making quite a number of hits on Bismarck. It was very frightening. I was just about twenty-years-old. I must admit I was scared to death, because I could see what our shells were doing to Bismarck. They were creating dreadful havoc.*'

9.04 am – Telling Damage

HMS *Norfolk*

The cruiser finally gets to join in, her own main weapons firing on the *Bismarck*. To John Ruffer, that first broadside of all eight 8-inch guns is 'louder than any thunderclap' creating 'tremendous concussion' and the *Norfolk* is given 'a long and ferocious shake'.

> '*There is a momentary cloud of swirling hot brown gas, and the 8-inch shells are on their way, at more than double the speed of sound.*'

One of the *Bismarck*'s 5.9-inch gun turrets blows up. Hundreds of men have been killed or wounded by now. More heavy shells hit the *Bismarck*; her forward turrets knocked out of action, one of them exploding.

The bridge and the gunnery command positions in the forward section of the *Bismarck* are being shredded, and it is the rapid-fire guns of both the *Norfolk* and the *Dorsetshire* that do much of the damage.

HMS *Rodney*

Len Nicholl is both awed and shocked by the destructive power being unleashed.

> *'I actually saw the back of the [Bismarck's] B turret explode when one of the shells hit her. It just flipped up in the air, spinning like a penny.'*

9.10 am – Torpedoes Away

Rodney's torpedo tubes are in action, too – white streaks of torpedoes heading towards *Bismarck* visible on the surface of the sea. At least one hits. Over the public address system Capt Dalrymple–Hamilton announces:

> *'We have made history in hitting another battleship with a torpedo.'*

9.12 am – Brain Knocked Out

KM *Bismarck*

As British shells rip through her superstructure, the *Bismarck* loses her ability to control her actions with the forward command post destroyed. The after-command post is also wiped out.

An 8-inch shell from the *Dorsetshire* hits the main gunnery control position. A German officer later describes this as achieving such a devastating impact it 'blew out *Bismarck*'s brains', removing her ability to fire with accuracy.

HMS *Dorsetshire*

George Bell can see that his ship is doing her share of damage, though the Germans still have plenty of fight left in them.

> *We fired 250 rounds, roughly, of 8-inch [during the battle]. The 8-inch guns were renowned then as some of the most accurate in the Navy and they were very, very effective. It was our guns that knocked out half of Bismarck's control systems. Suddenly we got a salvo over the top of us from Bismarck, but she didn't bother shooting at us anymore. Whether*

she was not capable or was otherwise engaged,
I don't know.'

9.19 am – Still Some Fight Left

HMS *Rodney*

Both *Bismarck*'s after turrets fire, and in the *Rodney*'s gunnery control position, Lt Cdr Crawford is also amazed to see shells from his own ship pass those of the German battleship coming the other way. *Bismarck*'s miss, but *Rodney*'s – joined by shells from *King George V*, *Dorsetshire* and *Norfolk* – hammer the enemy. Fire rages in *Bismarck*'s centre. Steam shoots out of jagged holes. Thick black smoke pours from her funnel.

HMS *King George V*

Peter Bridewell is finally in action as the range has reduced enough for the rapid-fire 5.25-inch secondary armament to open fire. Bridewell is being pushed to the limit supplying cordite charges to the men in the turret above his working chamber.

'I was standing on a platform pushing this
cordite up, which had been passed to us from
down below – picked up, then pushed up by us
through a chute. These cordite charges weighed

*something like 35 pounds. I found it very diffi-
cult after about five of them – bending down,
picking one up, standing up, pushing it up
through a chute... and getting a bit heavy.
And I noticed the fellow that was next to me,
serving the other gun, stood watching me.*

　'I said: "What's the matter with you?"

　*'He said: "My gun's stopped firing...
jammed." He pushed me out the way and said:
"Come on, I'll give it a go." And he helped
us... It was a very difficult job to do... doing
it every four seconds, with the gun firing.'*

HMS *Cossack*

While not involved in the action, destroyers are still
present on its margins, just in case they are needed.
From the *Cossack*, Ken Robinson has a clear view.

　*'Bismarck was getting hit regularly and
there was smoke, there was fire, there was
everythin'... oh God. We could see that the
Bismarck's battle flag was flying above the
smoke. That's one with a great big swastika.
We always flew a battle flag. You fly it on the
foremast. It's a White Ensign, but it's a big
one. I suppose they were the same and they had
this swastika flag on the mainmast and this
other great big naval ensign on the foremast.'*

9.25 am – Ripped Apart

KM *Bismarck*

The pride of the German fleet lurches drunkenly under each blow, adopting a list to port, huge pieces of superstructure flying off as she is taken apart. Inside the aft gunnery control position, Lt von Müllenheim-Rechberg is unable to target any British ships as his sighting optics are shattered.

HMS *Rodney*

Not since the Battle of Jutland a quarter of a century earlier has the Royal Navy been given such an opportunity to destroy a German battleship. In the spring of 1916, the Kaiser's High Seas Fleet escaped the trap, but, as Len Nicholl can see all too clearly, for the *Bismarck* there is to be no getting away.

> 'She was a sitting duck as far as we were concerned, and we closed on her, and we were firing these 16-inch shells. They were armour-piercing, and, instead of dropping down onto the ship, they were going through from one side to the other and possibly exploding out into the sea again. They were firing at too close a range, really. We did a tremendous amount of damage to her. I think the *Rodney's* six-inch shells

were doing as much. I was on the port side of the ship. We'd go up the port side firing at her, turn around and then the starboard side would have a go at firing. We would be in a bit of a lull on the port side. I saw Bismarck burning from stem to stern and she was a beautiful ship, beautiful schooner bows on her. Her stern was all nicely round off.'

9.27 am – *Bismarck*'s Fatal Flaws

KM *Bismarck*

The problem with the *Bismarck* is that looks can be deceptive.

On assuming power in 1933, the Nazis were so eager to create a new German battle fleet they adapted an old First World War design. The *Bismarck* had a modern profile, the latest weaponry and machinery, but also serious flaws.

Her rudders are inside her screws – which reduces the chances of steering effectively by propellers alone. While the accuracy and range of her 15-inch main armament is formidable, the *Bismarck*'s proliferation of different calibre anti-aircraft guns made it difficult to create an effective fire control system to utilise them to best effect. That is why she failed to shoot down a single aircraft during both Swordfish attacks.

Another major problem is that her citadel – the heavily armoured inner shell designed primarily to protect the engine rooms and also the magazines containing shells and cordite charges – does not offer adequate shielding for the command and control systems of the ship, which can be easily destroyed in a stand-up fight not only with enemy battleships but even heavy cruisers.

Nonetheless, the battle between the brand-new *Bismarck* and the elderly *Hood* in the Denmark Strait was most unequal – the British battlecruiser was designed and built during the First World War with her inter-war modernisation incomplete. She was never likely to be adequately protected to take on the *Bismarck*.

On 27 May though, the *Bismarck* faces a much tougher opponent in the *Rodney*. Although completed in the late 1920s, less manoeuvrable and slower than the *Bismarck*, the *Rodney* was designed with a formidable armoured citadel plus the heavily protected Octopoidal to protect her command and control systems. Also, even in 1941, she has the largest calibre main guns of any European battleship.

In the final showdown, once the *Bismarck* loses her ability to run away or even steer, she is robbed of her chief technical advantages over the British ship – greater speed and manoeuvrability. As Yves Dias sees from his position on the *Rodney*'s bridge, it is 'a slugging match ... slaughter'.

> 'We were getting nearer and nearer her, of course, and the range was closing. The closer we got the more destructive we became, until the Bismarck's guns were gradually knocked out one at a time. It was dreadful to see because the Bismarck was on fire. She was very much reduced in speed; shells were hitting her every time we fired. And we even fired broadsides at her, which was a terrible noise and it really was murder at the end because she couldn't defend herself anymore. Her sailors and crew were leaping overboard. The ship was on fire. It must have been absolute Hell onboard.'

To Len Nicholl and others also able to see everything up close, the enemy vessel seems almost within touching distance.

> 'Some of the lads on the guns said they could have hit her with potatoes, she was that close. I would say she was about 2,000 yards away from us, no more.'

For a battleship duel, it is point-blank range – the equivalent of two giants trying to land hits with claw hammers at arm's length.

9.30 am – Is *Bismarck* Trying to Surrender?

HMS *Rodney*

In the British battleship's gunnery director position, Tommy Byers is stunned by the horror unfolding as seen via his powerful optics.

'Very early in the battle men started jumping overboard from the Bismarck. They couldn't stand the heat and the shells bursting. One particular fellah stood on the top of B turret on the Bismarck waving his arms in semaphore. I saw this through my porthole and told the Gunnery Officer, Lt Cdr Crawford, and he says: "Oh, fuck 'em – don't want to know about any signal now."

'So, then she flew a black flag … from the top of the yard arm and that was "we want to parley with you". But Crawford wasn't having that.

'So then she started blinking with her semaphore, with her morse lamps on the yard arm – four lamps at a time. And he [Crawford] said: "I don't want to know, don't report any more of that…"

'So, she was for it. Then we saw this fellah semaphoring too and just at that moment a

16-inch shell hit the turret underneath him and
he just froze there.

'That was very sad, but it was her or us…'

Never in the history of modern warfare has a battle-ship surrendered in the heat of close combat, and the *Bismarck*'s colours are flying while some of her guns are still firing. Those attempting to capitulate may be taking unilateral action as they are in the parts of the ship that have proved most vulnerable.

They, quite understandably, want to save them-selves from the murderous enemy fire – but this may not be with the authority of their commanders (who are most probably already dead).

Having first been on target with the *Rodney*'s third salvo, including a hit on a turret, Crawford finds the enemy ship's accuracy has swiftly fallen away.

The *Bismarck*'s for'ard 15-inch turrets were knocked out 'quite early, but her after turrets went on firing.' As the *Rodney* closes the range down to 4,000 yards, the British battleship is 'pumping stuff into her pretty hard' relates Crawford.

'Through binoculars at very short range, where
you've got flat trajectory, you can see your
own shell going out away from you. I saw
three shells from Rodney going towards the
Bismarck. I saw two shells from Bismarck

coming towards us and passing in mid-air. It was an eerie sight, these things going at 2,000ft per second and looking as if the Bismarck shell was going down each barrel of the binoculars. They plunged into the sea a long way short.

'She kept up a desultory fire for a long time – a very, very brave action. Although we failed to sink her, we certainly knocked her about. She was on fire in many places, a lot of smoke. You could see the shells crumping against her side. But I don't honestly think that our ammunition was very good.

'On the 16-inch shell, you could either set the armour-piercing shell to delay or non-delay, according to your target. Normally against an armoured ship you always fired with the delay setting because you hoped to get the shell exploding inside the ship, where it'd do the maximum damage. And at one time the King George V... she was on the other side of Bismarck... reported that some of our shells were going through the ship and exploding outside. And I then gave the order for them to set the shells to non-delay, but I believe if our shells had been really efficient, we ought to have blown that ship up, however good her armour.

'Eventually, it was a rather bloody business. One had to go on, to sink the ship. But there were people, occasionally, whom I saw, a few of them, running aft and jumping over the side, while we were still engaging her – in fact, I think, while some of her turrets were still firing... Our job was to sink her ... as quickly as possible. We couldn't leave her floating about there and go away. And, of course, we were in the very difficult position that both ourselves and King George V were running extremely short of fuel...'

The stubborn resilience of the *Bismarck* is grinding her assailants down, and for those consigned to just being observers, it is probably worst of all. Crawford later ponders this terrible situation.

'Why the hell didn't she sink? One's sole aim, was to get the ship down [sunk] where she could no longer be a menace to anyone... I think some of the people who were just watching, who weren't actively doing [anything] had many more feelings than possibly I did, about the problem of whether we ought to be still firing at her. I had a job to do, which I had to get on with. I didn't really

have enough time to think very much about the
moral side of it.'

KM *Bismarck*

While sailors within the less well protected parts of
the superstructure are being torn to pieces by enemy
fire, the men inside the *Bismarck*'s heavily armoured
gun turrets carry on fighting. Within the citadel itself,
the oblivious engineers keep the lights and the essential systems supplied with electricity as if all is normal,
and, according to Otto Peters there is 'no trouble at
all with our engines'.

In the diesel electric room where he is stationed,
everything was 'perfect … And the turbines were
singing'.

> *'We had the noise of the diesel engines and*
> *the noise from the guns had to go through so*
> *many decks, so we couldn't hear anything of*
> *it, but we did notice [that] when the guns in*
> *[the Bismarck] fired … the ship would bend*
> *a little. If they shoot in a right angle from the*
> *ship, it bends to the opposite side…'*

As is common when such huge guns fire, the shock
vibrates through the hull, the entire ship in fact. It
can even move a battleship sideways in the water. In

his action station, Gerhard Junack notices that, after a while, reddish-yellow smoke is being emitted by a ventilator and so puts on his gas mask, noting:

> 'Obviously a serious fire was raging somewhere.'

Beyond the 15-inch gun turrets and machinery spaces, the slaughter in the *Bismarck* is terrible. One British shell carves through a compartment where medical staff are working on the wounded, killing everybody.

The impact of shell hits distorts hatches and doors so they can't be opened, and wreckage also blocks some exit routes. A rescue team tries to free sailors trapped in an ammunition magazine but when raging fires threaten to trigger an explosion, the order is given to flood the space. Everybody within it is drowned, but it buys some time for the *Bismarck*.

9.36 am – Bursting Like Eggs

HMS *Rodney*

Up in the Air Defence Position, Lt Campbell sweeps along the German battleship with his optics, watching as 6-inch shells from his own ship's secondary armament hit the *Bismarck*. They burst like eggs thrown against a wall. He sees shell after shell hit *Bismarck*'s bridge.

A yellow-hot flame consumes the forward superstructure of the enemy battleship. Campbell sees light signals on the *Bismarck*'s mast and wonders if the German ship is pleading to surrender. A shell slices through the mast, sending it toppling over the side into the sea.

HMS *Tartar*

For Ludovic Kennedy, aboard a tiny destroyer, watching as steel giants slug it out, 'it was a terrible sight'. He explains:

> '...*no sailor likes to see the death of another ship, friend or enemy, and there was this beautiful ... huge, powerful ship, absolutely battered into pieces ... first of all the foremast went over the side and then two of the guns – the foremast guns – one of them was drooping like a dead flower with the barrel of the gun split like a banana ... another one was pointing upwards to the sky and then we saw cracks in the superstructure and [through] the decks, fires were appearing, and that was pretty awful.*

'And, as I found out later, it was a terrible, terrible time for the Germans, they were suffering appalling casualties. And then right towards the end of the battle, we watched a little trickle of men begin running along to the end of the quarter deck – to the stern – and then jumping into the sea ... when I saw these little figures running down the Bismarck's quarter deck and jumping into the sea off the stern, it was really brought home to one that it was human beings that one was fighting against.'

9.40 am – Who Has Command of the Ship?

KM *Bismarck*

Now all *Bismarck*'s big guns are silent, though some of the 5.9-inch secondary weapons are firing sporadically.

Gas and smoke seeps into the aft gunnery control position, forcing von Müllenheim-Rechberg and his team to pull on gas masks.

The phone rings, and von Müllenheim-Rechberg answers it to be told by another officer in the forward fire control station that it is being evacuated due to smoke and gas. Before von Müllenheim-Rechberg can ask if the Captain and Admiral are still alive, and if anyone is giving orders, the officer rings off.

Von Müllenheim-Rechberg begins telephoning around the ship, trying to raise somebody in any part of the vessel, seeking to find out what is happening. *Bismarck* shudders to yet more hits.

Someone picks up the phone in the damage control centre. Von Müllenheim-Rechberg demands:

'Who has command of the ship?'

The man tells him the damage control centre is being abandoned, that he is the last man in there and slams the phone down.

9.45 am – She Won't Go Down

Bismarck is nothing but wreckage, a charnel house, but still nobody strikes her ensign, the internationally recognised signal for surrender. There is no feasible way for the British to capture her – certainly not with Luftwaffe bombers expected at any moment and U-boats known to be nearby. She must be sunk, and so the British ships continue pouring fire into her.

Three 16-inch shells cut through the sky, supersonic blurs as they hit the *Bismarck*, causing shock ripples on the surface of the sea. They penetrate deep, an explosion ripping apart a forward 15-inch gun turret, throwing up sheets of flame. *Rodney*'s gunnery officer decides to fire all nine of the ship's 16-inch guns at once, a dangerous proposition, as the shock could severely damage his own vessel. All of those shells hit *Bismarck*, some going right through and skipping away, like glowing tennis balls. Those who can see what is going on from *Rodney*, including Len Nicholl, are increasingly sickened. No matter how many shells slam into *Bismarck* – no matter how many holes are punched into and through her – she still won't sink.

> 'It was dreadful. When I saw the kind of damage we were doing to the ship I thought: "What a life it is, this War!?" To think you are killing each other, smacking in massive great shells like that. And she was a brilliant ship, but what damage would she have done had she got away into the Atlantic?'

Strangely, while others have spotted what they take to be signs of surrender attempts, Len sees no such evidence or even German sailors leaping overboard.

> 'Though I had a monocular eye glass, I never saw any persons running around. Not on the decks at all, or any part of the ship, and I had a good view, a very close up view. I never saw a soul on there. Some people say they saw them in the water, but I never saw anybody.'

9.52 am – Punch Drunk

Rodney fires all nine 16-inch guns again, with six of the shells, hitting *Bismarck*, making more holes in the already ravaged ship, killing dozens of men. Like a punch-drunk boxer, *Bismarck* reels from the hits, white-hot pieces of metal spinning off her and twirling through the air.

Two hundred men entombed by warped hatches within the forward canteen compartment are ripped to pieces, creating 'mountains of flesh and bone' according to one German sailor.

9.52 am – Still Being Punished

Rodney launches torpedoes, as the *Dorsetshire* closes in too. The cruiser's 8-inch guns bark as she turns to port. Shells from the *Bismarck*'s 5.9-inch secondary armament guns curve overhead but splash harmlessly, well away from the British cruiser.

10.00 am – Furious Onlookers

HMS *Ark Royal* / Swordfish

The young aviators, including Terry Goddard, were earlier able to finally launch from *Ark* with their spirits high. What they find at the scene of battle takes the edge off any triumphalism they may have felt on take-off. 'It wasn't raining on the morning of the 27th but the weather was still ugly,' recalls Terry Goddard.

> '…with the ship [Ark Royal] still pitching up and down, though not so much green water over the bows. The atmosphere was much more relaxed, almost carefree, which was down to the fact that we'd all survived. Nobody had been shot down. We really did want to go again. I think we wanted to get there before the Home Fleet did. Then we were delayed about two hours, partly because of weather.
>
> 'As we approached Bismarck, the weather was better. We were at about 2,000ft. Bismarck was surrounded by battleships, cruisers and destroyers. She was being mercilessly pounded. Her A turret was gone. The after turrets were still firing. She was steaming at about seven knots, if that. The bridge was gone … there was just a big black hole billowing black smoke. She was a mess, and the gunfire was just cease-less… pounding her, pounding her, pounding her…'

Fearing these might be enemy planes, King George V's anti-aircraft guns open fire on the Swordfish but miss. Hoping they can make a contribution to putting

Bismarck under, *Ark Royal*'s Swordfish circle overhead, but are ordered to stay away. Their aircrews watch the gruesome spectacle below reach its terrible climax.

> '*We asked permission to attack and were told, no, we couldn't attack, that we should stay away. Now, why do you suppose that was? There was no way the Fleet Air Arm with its torpedoes was going to sink the Bismarck. C-in-C [Tovey] was going to sink the Bismarck with guns. No aircraft was going to do it. It was really irritating, cruising around with a bunch of torpedoes still hung up and not being allowed to attack. The subsequent reason given was they didn't want us to be subjected to gunfire. There was no bloody reason the Home Fleet couldn't have stopped firing while we went in and attacked.*'

10.11 am – 'Oh God, Why Don't They Stop?'

HMS *Rodney*

Lt Campbell prays for the slaughter to end. Large pieces of the *Bismarck*'s stern are blown off, tumbling and twirling through the air, hitting the sea with enormous splashes. More smoke and flame pours out of *Bismarck*.

Campbell calls out:

'Oh. God, why don't they stop?'

On the British battleship's bridge, Yves Dias suspects the *Rodney* is harming herself.

> *'Every time we fired a broadside, apparently there was such a shaking up below decks. We really shouldn't have done anymore broadsides at all. There was mirrors broken, there was crockery all over the place, and apparently a complete shambles. We were hitting Bismarck almost with every shot, yet Bismarck never hit us properly once. Of course we're not psychic – at least I'm not – and I didn't know that we wouldn't be hit. I was just waiting, expecting the whole time to be hit, so I can't say I was terribly brave. In fact, I wasn't brave at all, but it was so spectacular to see this beautiful ship on fire from bow to stern and sailors jumping overboard. You sort of felt sorry for them.'*

KM *Bismarck*

Some of *Bismarck*'s hatches are so buckled and crumpled, men wearing lifejackets cannot squeeze through. According to one member of the crew, by now the exits are 'blocked by a struggling mass of men, whom officers could no longer control.' Those who do manage to make it outside, aim to dash across the deck and throw themselves overboard.

Blinded and choked by smoke and flames, some instead tumble through large shell holes into the inferno below.

Some wait until there is a momentary lull in the firing and then make their bid to reach the sea. Those who sprint in a blind panic are, according to one of *Bismarck*'s men, 'blown to pieces'.

Some sailors refuse to leave whatever shelter they can find, screaming:

'We are not going out!'

They prefer the heat and fumes inside the ship to the hellfire on the upper deck. Others tell them to get out of the way so they can at least try and escape.

10.13 am – Seemingly Defenceless

HMS *Rodney*

The British battleship shudders as another salvo of 16-inch shells is hurled at the *Bismarck*, hitting and triggering large explosions. One of the *Rodney*'s chaplains comes onto the bridge, standing to one side of Yves Dias and next to Capt Dalrymple-Hamilton. Dias sees the man of God recoil from the slaughter being inflicted on the seemingly defenceless German ship.

> 'The bridge wasn't all that huge, and my binoculars were sort of fairly near the conning place where the Captain was seated beside his compass. The Padre said to the Captain that it should stop.
>
> 'He said: "You are firing shells at a ship that can't reply."
>
> 'And the Captain, said: "You go and mind your own business and get off my bridge."
>
> 'Shortly after that we did, in fact, cease fire.'

Capt Dalrymple-Hamilton is just as sickened as the Padre, but as a capital ship captain under orders to dispose of such a deadly enemy vessel, he has to make sure she is utterly destroyed.

A major problem is that *Rodney* disembarked all her HE shells in Britain due to the forthcoming refit. She is carrying only Armour-Piercing (AP) shells. These do not penetrate and explode but often go in one side of the *Bismarck* – carving a terrible path of destruction through metal and flesh – before punching out the other. Dalrymple-Hamilton feels it is increasingly a futile effort, so he orders his ship's bombardment to cease.

Len Nicholl is grateful for an end to the din and the nauseous smoke generated by the guns. The range is now so close, it is difficult to lay them on target anyway.

> *'It was a waste of time. It is just impossible to fire the guns with that depression on them. The guns wouldn't depress low enough to hit her.'*

10.15 am – Silent Guns

HMS *Dorsetshire*

Capt Martin's cruiser also stops firing, the ears of her sailors humming. The hot gun barrels show bare steel where the paint has been seared and blasted off. The thunder and roar of weapons is replaced by the hiss of the ocean washing down the hull of the high-sided ship.

Capt Martin and the men of *Dorsetshire* silently look on as *Bismarck* rises and falls, the leaping sea washing away small black dots of men and momentarily dousing flames. These shoot up again each time the *Bismarck* rises. There is a kettledrum roll as the fleet flagship's 14-inch guns fire. The noise of heavy shells ripping through the air like distant summer thunder is followed by mute shell splashes around the *Bismarck* and a new eruption of smoke and flame.

From the Admiral's Bridge of the Home Fleet flagship, Admiral Tovey scans the dying enemy giant, which is 'on fire fore and aft and wallowing more heavily every moment.'…

> *'Men could be seen jumping overboard preferring death by drowning in the stormy sea to the appalling effects of our fire. I was confident that the Bismarck could never get back to harbour and that it was only a matter of hours before she would sink.'*

KM *Bismarck*

The telephone buzzes in Junack's compartment and he picks it up to find Lehmann on the other end, who tells him:

> *'Prepare for sinking.'*

This is the last order he receives before 'all transmission of orders collapsed'.

A Petty Officer that Junack sends to find out what is going on does not return. Junack decides to issue orders for the explosive charges to be 'connected' in order to scuttle the ship, by blowing out the cooling water intakes and so allowing water to gush into the ship.

Before leaving he ensures that bulkhead doors are open to enable effective flooding of the machinery spaces. Junack tells his men to leave their action stations and then follows them up through the vessel.

10.21 am – They Were Only Young Lads

HMS *King George V*

Admiral Tovey orders the Home Fleet flagship to cease-fire and decides the main British units should withdraw. With fuel scarce, it is time to head back to Britain and remove the Royal Navy's own battleships from potential revenge.

Not content to let the enemy battleship take hours to sink of her own accord, Tovey orders any ships 'still with torpedoes to use them on *Bismarck*'.

HMS *Rodney*

As his ship leaves the scene, 21-year-old stoker Alfred Brimacombe climbs up through the vessel from an engineering space, where he has been keeping vital machinery going throughout the battle.

Born in Plymouth's historic Barbican quarter, from where Elizabethan seadogs once sailed to explore the world and terrify England's enemies, the sea is in Brimacombe's blood.

For someone who has spent much of his life on the ocean wave in small boats, being one of *Rodney*'s stokers – spending his time in dark, hot narrow passageways and gloomy machinery spaces – is a strange kind of troglodyte existence.

> '*You went right down into the bottom of the ship where there were no lights, with just a torch to find your way and once you had done your job with the pumps and the valves you went back up.*'

Prior to the battle, as they descended to their action stations in the engine room, a grizzled Chief Petty Officer told Brimacombe they would be lucky to get out of it alive.

Now Brimacombe is heading for a compartment off the boat deck where there is a tank of oil that feeds the galleys. The cooks want to start preparing a hot meal now the Action is over. Brimacombe's job is to turn a valve so the oil can feed through to the stoves and ovens. Doing this, he sees something he will never be able to erase from his memory.

> '*The Rodney came down around where all the men was in the water and we just went by*

*them. I noticed one of them waving, wanting
to be picked up. I didn't feel good, like, and
I know they was enemies, but they were only
young lads, very young lads. It was either they
or us wasn't it? I don't know if anyone picked
them up, but it was a hell of a lot of men in
the water... a hell of a lot.'*

10.22 am – Abandon Ship?

KM *Bismarck*

Having received no orders to abandon ship, but real-
ising the *Bismarck* is done for, von Müllenheim-
Rechberg, has waited until all the firing has stopped
before leading his team out onto the upper deck. He
sees the *Rodney* standing off, the black muzzles of her
big guns pointing straight at him.

Meanwhile, Junack has made it to the Battery
Deck, where the secondary guns are mounted, and
finds a situation radically different from the 'lower
decks [which] were brilliantly lit up; a peaceful mood
prevailed such as that on a Sunday afternoon in
port...'

Now he is in darkness, lit only by 'the red glow
from numerous fires' creating smoke and choking
fumes, and with wreckage strewn all over the place.
Anarchy reigns as men run here and there to no
purpose.

Junack thinks he will not survive.

Von Müllenheim-Rechberg is appalled by the carnage surrounding him, including one of the 15-inch gun turrets he commanded wrecked, blackened from a hit and with one of its guns shattered by an enemy hit. He gazes across the water at HMS *Rodney*, her guns 'still pointing mistrustfully' at *Bismarck*. As the ship begins to capsize, von Müllenheim-Rechberg orders his men to salute 'fallen comrades' and then jump over the side. More than 700 of the *Bismarck*'s men are in the water, but there are few life-rafts, and so most of them stand little chance of surviving.

10.25 am – Situation Check

Force H

Having been ordered to hold Force H back and keep his battle-cruiser flagship HMS *Renown* out of harm's way, Admiral Somerville sends old friend Jack Tovey a signal enquiring what's going on.

Have you disposed of the enemy?

Three minutes later Tovey responds that he has suspended action due to the fuel situation.

Tovey subsequently sends Somerville a signal that later will be taken out of context by some to indicate the British were unable to sink the *Bismarck*. The controversial signal reads:

I could not sink Bismarck with gunfire.

Knowing that Somerville will have been reading signals on the Admiralty net, the Home Fleet boss assumed the Force H commander would understand the proper context. Somerville will have already noted the earlier general signal that ships 'still with torpedoes' were required to fire them into *Bismarck*.

This would hasten the process of sinking already begun by British guns and earlier torpedo hits. Tovey will explain in his official report on the battle that this signal's aim was 'to ensure that he [Somerville] should take any steps which might help to hasten her sinking' but, Tovey admitted somewhat sheepishly, 'when intercepted by others [read by other people on the Admiralty signals net], it may have caused some misunderstanding.'

Somerville's intervention is not needed anyway, for a warship still at the scene of battle had already accepted the task.

10.26 am – The Coup De Grace

HMS *Dorsetshire*

As the heavy cruiser moves in for the kill, from her bridge George Bell sees the final blows delivered.

> *'We went in until she was about a mile-and-a-half away from the Dorsetshire. Where I was standing was the torpedo officer, alongside his controls and firing mechanism. When he got the order from the Captain, I witnessed the torpedoes being fired. He fired two torpedoes at her, hitting her with both. Obviously the two torpedoes were not going to sink her, so the captain decided to go 'round the bows of the ship and fire more. We weren't quite so sure all of Bismarck's guns were going to be out of action on the other side … fortunately they were. We closed the range again and were going to fire two, three, four torpedoes, but when we fired the third one, it hit, and she started to roll over. I saw her keel from stem to stern as she rolled over completely and disappeared under the waves.'*

10.36 am – Who Has Won?

U-74

The hydrophone operator aboard this boat has picked up the unmistakable sound of a ship sinking, along with large explosions, but is it British or German?

HMS *Ark Royal* / Swordfish

The final moments of the *Bismarck* are witnessed by the *Ark Royal*'s aviators circling overhead. Terry Goddard thinks it is one of the worst things he has ever seen.

> *'It was ugly. In my opinion you might almost classify it as murder. Just ceaseless bombardment. Bismarck wasn't firing. Sure, her colours were still flying, but Bismarck, for the last 15 minutes of the shelling, was out of control. They were jumping in the water, which was full of hundreds of bobbing sailors. The ship was ablaze from head to stern, the forward turrets were hanging over the side. The rear turrets were pointing to the skies. The bridge was gone. There was just a great big hole. She was listing about 40 or 50 degrees to starboard and then she started to go down by the stern. Just before she rolled over, up came the bow as*

if to say "up yours", and, amidst a great big mass of bubbles, she went down.

'It was a dirty, dirty affair in my opinion at the end. I knew that Bismarck had to be sunk, but this onslaught really brought on feelings of revulsion – it was too much, far too much. Nothing could assuage those feelings … it was something I am never going to be able to forget. It was something I could not believe was happening. I had been imbued with the British spirit, British fairness and so on… it wasn't British, it was far from it. It really was pitiful.

'This great ship – make no mistake Bismarck was a magnificent ship – and at the end she was an ugly pathetic burning hulk with hundreds of dead bodies and the remainder of them bobbing helplessly in cold ugly Atlantic Ocean. A pathetic end.'

He wished the Swordfish had been permitted to help put the *Bismarck* out of her misery and end things sooner.

'Ultimately, even at the end, when C-in-C called up and said, "if anybody has any torpedoes left please go in and torpedo the Bismarck", we were not allowed to

> *attack. Fifteen aircraft torpedoes were jettisoned uselessly into the sea. Guns reigned supreme in the Royal Navy and they were supplemented by aircraft. Guns were going to sink Bismarck. Ships were going to sink the Bismarck, not bloody aircraft.'*

From another Swordfish circling overhead, 'Splash' Carver also gazes down on the shrapnel-lashed panorama of destruction.

> *'Bismarck was finished. She was a blazing wreck. I think I later described her as a "cauldron of fire", making a few knots through the water, but a bit of a list on... I saw one torpedo [from the Dorsetshire] hit her aft, or just by the quarterdeck, and she immediately started to list to port, and went right over ... taking about 15 seconds I suppose.*
>
> *'I heaved a sigh of relief and my first reaction was: "Thank God we've avenged the Hood."*
>
> *'My second thought was: "What a gallant fight that the Germans had put up against impossible odds."'*

Remarkably it appears that *Bismarck*'s Kapitän Lindemann somehow survives to the end but chooses to stay with his ship.

Junior rating Rudolf Römer, who is already in the sea, watches the captain and his messenger go forward through the *Bismarck*'s forecastle wreckage to the bow where they salute at attention.

To Römer it appears Lindemann then gestures for the messenger to abandon ship, but the man stays with him. As the ship begins to turn over, the messenger falls into the sea, with Lindemann climbing over railings to walk down the hull as *Bismarck* continues rolling.

Lindemann is visible for a few more moments, again saluting, before dropping into the sea to be sucked down by the *Bismarck*'s death plunge.

HMS *Maori*

Innes Hamilton has watched the *Bismarck* being 'pounded to scrap metal by our ships... She looked like a magnificent, wounded elephant.'...

> *'She was, of course, probably the most marvellous ship ever built – the Germans know how to build a ship and she was the finest example. Absolutely magnificent ... one of the finest products ever from a shipbuilding yard.'*

Although the men of the *Maori* are 'full of admiration' for the fight the Germans had put up, 'it was inevitable, in spite of her strength, that *Bismarck* would go down.'

> *'We had no inkling of course whether the Germans themselves had opened the sea cocks or whether she had in fact sunk due to gunfire. It was a sad sight. But, of course, the Royal Navy had to sink the Bismarck. There was no question, after she had sunk the Hood… we'd have done anything.'*

HMS *Rodney*

With the battle concluding, Lt Cdr Crawford leaves the main gunnery control position and goes down to the charthouse for a chat with a fellow officer, and he 'came out just in time to see the last of *Bismarck*'s keel, as she turned over' and looking like 'a giant whale' in her death throes. Crawford feels a whole range of emotions.

> *'Thank goodness she's gone, but she was the finest ship that I ever saw. She was a marvellous-looking ship, and a wonderful fighting ship – there's no doubt about it. She was a really very beautiful ship, comparable in a way to the beauty of the Hood, which in her day was the most beautiful ship. But of course*

Hood was an old ship and had certain terrible weaknesses...

'I think in the [Rodney's] lower deck there was great jubilation... But a great number of us, I think, felt that it was sad that it had to be like that. A gallant ship had gone, and a lot of gallant people had gone, although they were our enemies... our feelings were slightly tinged with a bit of sadness...

'I think one had a pretty hearty dislike for their submarines generally, because they were the people who caused so much slaughter among our merchant ships... I don't think one felt any particular form of sort of hatred [for the Germans in general, but] I mean they were our enemies and we had to get the better of them.'

The admiration of the *Bismarck*'s beauty by William Crawford, as well as by Innes Hamilton and Ludovic Kennedy, is a curious paradoxical facet of the battle – praise for the lines and firepower of the enemy vessel they were determined to destroy, not least for killing 1,415 shipmates aboard the *Hood*, which remains to this day the greatest loss of life in a single Royal Navy vessel.

Below the surface beauty, the *Bismarck*'s flaws also extended to poor quality of construction in her stern.

When she turned over to take her death plunge, it sheered away. No ship is invincible or so perfectly constructed that it is invulnerable to sinking – not the *Titanic*, nor the *Hood*, and certainly not the *Bismarck*.

HMS *Norfolk*

Aboard the heavy cruiser as she sails away from the scene of battle – more than 1,700 miles and almost four days since her lookouts first laid eyes on the *Bismarck* in the Denmark Strait – an exhausted Lt John Ruffer notes that someone is 'drinking champagne' to salute the victory. His final observation is typically terse but says it all.

> *High morale. FATIGUE.*

Kriegsmarine Group West HQ

Having picked up on news wires claims that *Bismarck* has been sunk, the Kriegsmarine Group West HQ tries to check their veracity, so sends a wireless signal to Lütjens.

> *Reuter reports: Bismarck sunk. Report situation immediately.*

There is only silence, which is confirmation in itself.

Hand of Mercy

Back in London

In a temporary debating chamber in Church House, central London – a stand-in House of Commons, due to a recent Luftwaffe fire-bombing raid that damaged the Palace of Westminster – Winston Churchill has been explaining how the *Hood* was lost in action against the *Bismarck* on 24 May.

As he details the subsequent pursuit by the Royal Navy, the PM is praying for some good news to provide the perfect conclusion.

Churchill tells MPs the Home Fleet has engaged *Bismarck*. The outcome is not yet known, but surely must see the Nazi battleship destroyed.

He sits down and listens to an MP asking how was it *Hood* had not been modernised to better protect her against the enemy's gunfire?

Churchill explains she had been properly refitted in 1931, but further strengthening was not possible amid all her war duties.

The MPs move on to other business, but the PM's Parliamentary Private Secretary, Brendan Bracken, pushes his way through a crowd of MPs and into the chamber. A note is passed along to Churchill, who stands up again, begging the indulgence of the Speaker. He reveals:

> *'I have just received news that the Bismarck is sunk.'*

The London-based correspondent of the *New York Times* later tells his readers via a 'special cable' that HMS *Hood*, 'blown up by an "unlucky hit" from the *Bismarck*, was thus avenged.'

Meanwhile, in the Atlantic...

Survivors

Hundreds of the German battleship's men have been fighting to stay alive while praying for rescue.

On being given the order to exit the machinery spaces, Otto Peters made his way up through eight decks – well protected within the battleship's armoured citadel – to the Battery Deck, an odyssey in itself. Near the end of his journey he entered a compartment where 'lights and everything was out', and it had been partially flooded.

> *'Then we got a hit in that room where I was – a heavy hit … the ship made a little jump, but I was lucky, I wasn't hit. I tried to open this door. Everything was dark, and got it open about one feet [sic] wide. And I could see daylight. I couldn't get through the door, so I threw away my leather jacket to get through. So, I came to the upper deck.'*

Emerging, Peters was pleased to escape the heat down below, but the sights that greeted him as he pulled on a life vest were horrific.

> *'Hundreds and hundreds of shipmates were lying there in blood. The turrets were crooked, and three quarters of the ship was underneath the sea already. I saw the ship, almost everything was destroyed. I tried to stay as long as possible on the upper deck, but the waves were going over the ship … and I tried to keep away from wood, which can kill you because it's going with the wave and it has force … lying on the deck of the ship, I was able to catch [a hold of] something, but when the second wave came, it took me out of the ship…'*

After gathering some men and steadying their nerves – telling them to 'stay together in the water, keep calm, don't give up hope, and be careful when interrogated by the enemy' – Junack leads them in a 'triple "Sieg Heil!".' Only then does he tell them to jump overboard.

However, there is no safety in large numbers when it comes to surviving in the sea after a ship has been sunk. Panic can easily spread among people so despairing of salvation. They may thrash in the water and drown, taking you down with them. Staying at a distance alone, or with just a few shipmates you know, is a much better option, and so Otto Peters went solo.

> 'I saw three big groups swimming, and I thought: "Don t go there". Because one cannot help each other as long as one is in the sea. So, I kept on my own. On the sea was oil and so I was pretty determined I should not swallow this. I tried to get away from the ship as quick as possible – and it was raining and stormy – but anyway, one tries to live. I saw the ship going down – it went down, upside down [with] the screws [going under] first. Even today I can see it in my head.
>
> 'So, after this I swam. I knew I could not swim to Germany – impossible! – so I tried to float on the water without moving more than a

little bit, but if one doesn't move, one gets cold.
I wasn't married at the time, but I had a girl
in Hamburg, and I thought: "I must see her
again! I must see her again! I won't go down!"
That was going on in my head while I was in
the water.'

Some of the *Bismarck* survivors believed when they saw an enemy vessel nearby that it was not there to rescue them but rather to finish them off. Peters considered it a chance worth taking if it meant escaping a terrible death from drowning or exposure.

'I tried to swim to this ship, and I could see
it very clear – the Union Jack – so it must be
a British ship. And I thought: "Now they're
going to kill us in the water."

'Coming closer to the ship I saw they had
ropes down and so I thought to myself: "Now
they're going to pick us up". Maybe I was one
of the first reaching the ship… So, I just took
a rope,, and the ship was not moving. When
the waves reach the ship – in this case it was
the British cruiser Dorsetshire – they go up the
ship.

'So, I took a rope and the wave brought me
up all the way, and when the climax came, I
dropped back down. This happened three times

and the fourth time I put the rope in between my legs, made a loop and kept it this way. When the wave reached the climax again, I hit the steel [hull of the Dorsetshire] and I was grabbed by British shipmates. They threw me like a pig on the upper deck so they could rescue others. They had no time to take me to a cabin or wherever.'

A few German sailors, indoctrinated to believe the enemy will kill them rather than provide rescue, actually swim away while one officer shoots himself with a pistol.

HMS *Dorsetshire*

Aboard the *Dorsetshire*, George Bell was sent down by Capt Martin to see the Commander – second in command of the cruiser – with instructions for picking up the *Bismarck*'s men. The sea was too rough to launch boats, so they would have to be brought aboard by other means and as swiftly as possible.

'We received a signal from the admiral to collect survivors. We did it because they were seamen doing their job of work and we had done our job, which was to sink the Bismarck. We weren't far from Bismarck, extremely close, and

scrambling nets and various bits of equipment was made ready to help get survivors aboard. There was no question at all in our minds that they were sailors who wanted saving.

'Well, of course a County Class cruiser has got a lot of freeboard, so they needed quite a lot of assistance in getting up there. I saw quite a few of the Germans being pulled out the water but most of my time was spent delivering messages quickly and then back up onto the bridge.

'A 10,000-ton cruiser like Dorsetshire has no anti-submarine detecting equipment and is a tempting target if you happen to be in a U-boat. The first thing on Captain Martin's mind was the safety of his own ship, and there was a warning from one of the lookouts on the bridge that they'd seen what was possibly some evidence – a sort of a haze – of a submarine in the area. The Captain turned around to me and ordered me to go and see the Commander on the quarterdeck to tell him to throw all available rafts over the side. He would be getting underway immediately to clear the area.

'And that is what happened, though we were still able to pick up what survivors we could. I've seen bits in library books – and

> *somebody's actually underlined and made a comment – saying we left German survivors in the water, deliberately stopped picking them up. Captain Martin could not afford to risk his ship and the Germans understood that. There were 750 men in Captain Martin's own crew that were very much on his mind.'*

Those saved by the *Dorsetshire* included Lt von Müllenheim-Rechberg who remonstrated with Capt Martin for leaving a lot of *Bismarck*'s men in the sea. The German received a stern response from the cruiser CO, who told him that the safety of his own ship and her men was his top priority. Von Müllenheim-Rechberg had to concede the point.

During the time the British cruiser was stopped, one of her own midshipman jumped over the side to help wounded Germans scramble up the ship's side. Bell would be by the Captain's side when Midshipman Joe Brooks was ticked off for this deed.

> *'The Captain gave him quite a good talking to. Of course as Dorsetshire had to leave, he risked being left behind. Captain Martin told him quite bluntly he shouldn't have done it. He'd been trying to rescue a German who was badly injured get out the water and fortunately he was able to get back onboard before we left.'*

Having failed to pick up the War Log of Admiral Lütjens during the day, *U-74* arrived in the area before 9.00 pm on 27 May and pulled three of the *Bismarck*'s men from the sea. The hunt for the *Bismarck* survivors continued into 28 May and *U-48* reported to the U-boat forces headquarters in France at 9.25 am that she had found 'a number of floating corpses, a paravane [mine sweeping device] and wreckage...'

With other U-boats ordered to assist in the search, the Italian submarine *Barbarigo* – heading back to Bordeaux – was also asked to help.

The cruiser *Canarias* of neutral Spain's navy also got involved. More wreckage was found in the afternoon, by both *U-48* and *U-74*, but, as noted in the U-boat war log:

> *The search was broken off at dusk on orders of C.-in-C. Navy, no further reports of successful rescue operations having been received by evening.*

KM *Sachsenwald*

Not long after midnight on 29 May, two more survivors were found – in a life-raft – by the weather ship *Sachsenwald*, a large, converted fishing boat, which had been trying to coordinate her efforts with the U-boats.

The *Sachsenwald* had been riding the stormy Atlantic for 50 days in order to gain weather reports to be passed on to the German naval headquarters for operations against British convoys.

Commanded by Leutnant W Schütte, a veteran trawlerman, *Sachsenwald* was ordered to somehow assist *Bismarck* in the early hours of 27 May. Making speed, but steaming straight into rough seas, the ship was advised to hold her position at 6.00 am, then ordered to head for a position close to *Bismarck*. That evening she was strafed by a British aircraft but avoided damage.

Leutnant Schütte recorded sighting 'thin oil streaks' and then 'an empty tin container of a German gasmask' followed by 'numerous bodies still in their lifejackets, pieces of wreckage and empty lifejackets'. He also established first contact with the U-boats. 'We crisscrossed the debris field,' reported Schütte.

Exchanging messages with *U-48* via semaphore flags to avoid making giveaway radio transmissions, *Sachsenwald* headed south – finding only bodies – and then north.

At 10.35 pm, as dusk fell, three red signal rockets were spotted around three nautical miles away. 'I could now make out through the night binoculars a raft containing two men,' reported Schütte.

> *'After we came within shouting range, the first question [to us] was: "Are you Germans!?" With the answer of "yes", both [men on the raft] yelled as loud a hurrah as their strengths allowed."'*

The exhausted survivors were lifted aboard, helped up rope ladders by the weather ship's men. Their wet clothing was removed, and they were 'given dry, warm clothes' while 'the saltwater was washed from their faces and they were laid down on a berth'.

They turned out to be Otto Maus and Walter Lorenzen. They explained there were other survivors in a raft nearby. Resuming the search at daylight, despite the heavy seas, more empty lifejackets and piece of debris were spotted. In the evening, only an empty rubber raft was found, which Maus identified as belonging to the *Bismarck*.

HMS *Maori*

The destroyer HMS *Maori* picked up a further 25 survivors. Along with the *Dorsetshire*'s 86 and those saved by *U-74* and *Sachsenwald* that made 116 men out of *Bismarck*'s 2,365 complement rescued. The

Maori's Lt Innes Hamilton found the Germans his ship plucked from the sea to be 'of two distinct types':

> *'Many of them were exactly the same as our sailors. They were professional sailors, extremely good at their job – doing what they were taught, fighting for their country – honourable people and were glad to be rescued. They were taken below by our sailors and the oil fuel washed out of their eyes. They were given hot drinks and whatever, along with clean clothes, with affection by our sailors. It was one lot of professionals talking to another lot of professionals and looking after them in their distress.*
>
> *'On the other hand, there were a few members of the Hitler Youth who had recently, obviously, been recruited into the German Navy who came onboard and looked at the White Ensign and spat on the deck. They did not receive the same treatment; I will leave it at that. I would rather not elaborate…*
>
> *'We had great affection for the old sweats from the German crew who were doing their job just like we were and had been through hell.'*

When the *Maori* heard of a U-boat in close proximity, she had to quit the scene. Hamilton recalled that George Clark, a rating who could speak German, was asked to convey the terrible news to the *Bismarck* survivors still struggling in the sea.

> 'He shouted to the unfortunate German sailors, that we were picking up out of the water that they must swim away from the ship because we had to go ahead with our screws going flat out because we had received a U-boat warning… It is something I will never forget.'

Still at Sea

The three survivors of HMS *Hood* – Ted Briggs, Bill Dundas, and Robert Tilbrook – were at sea when the *Bismarck* was destroyed.

Having been landed at Reykjavik in Iceland by the *Electra*, they received a check-up in a British military hospital. A padre also spoke with each man, taking down his personal details, sending telegrams to families to convey the good news. 'We were in Iceland for a couple of days, and we came home in one of the troop ships operating back and forth from Iceland,' said Briggs.

'And we were put in a cabin, the three of us and told we could have anything we wanted but mustn't talk to anyone. And it was on the morning of 27 May that the first mate came in to tell us that Bismarck had been sighted and was in action with King George V.'

Once ashore in Scotland, the *Hood* survivors boarded a train for London, where, Briggs recalled, they were taken to the Admiralty to be interviewed by the Second Sea Lord and Chief of Naval Personnel, Admiral William 'Jock' Whitworth. He had been the previous Battle Cruiser Squadron boss, leaving the *Hood* in early May 1941 on handing over to Admiral Holland.

'He was very keen to see us, and he remembered me because once, when he was walking up and down the admiral's bridge [of Hood] in the middle of the night, I was charging across [with a message] and bumped into him and knocked him flat on his backside.

'And so, he now looked at me and said: "I know you, don't I?"

'I said: "Yes."

'He said, "Alright" and, patting me, added, "Get your hair cut, you'll be all right."

And then he said: "Well, what are your orders?"

'And Midshipman Dundas said: "We've been told to report to our depots when we leave here."

'He turned around to his chief of staff and said: "No, send these boys straight home, on leave." He also said: "We'll send for you when the court of inquiry comes up." And that was it.'

HMS *Dorsetshire*

Otto Peters was meanwhile still aboard the *Dorsetshire* on his way to spend five years as a Prisoner of War in Britain and Canada.

'We were three days on the Dorsetshire and on the second day, I think it was the second day — the captain [of the cruiser, Benjamin Martin] came through. He talked to us and he said that during First World War he was in German captivity and was well treated. He told us: "Please let me know your names." So, we gave him our names, because it was no secret anymore. He told us: "I'll send these names by wireless to the Red Cross."

> *'During that time my brother was a wire-*
> *less operator in the army, and he picked up*
> *my name. Three days since the sinking of the*
> *Bismarck my parents knew that I was rescued.'*

One of the survivors aboard the *Dorsetshire* died of his wounds and was buried at sea with full honours, though not with a Nazi flag draping his hammock-encased body before it was tipped over the side, but rather the German naval ensign.

The Home Fleet

The various British ships departed the scene of the battle with their sailors and Royal Marines thanking their lucky stars they had not been in *Bismarck*. Aboard *Dorsetshire*, George Bell thought he had just experienced the most intense few hours of his short life.

> *'We just happened to be the cruiser with the*
> *torpedoes available when the admiral wanted*
> *Bismarck sinking. She had to be sunk. We*
> *knew full well there was no way we could allow*
> *U-boats or anybody else to come and help her*
> *back to port.'*

As the *Cossack* steamed north through the Irish Sea, Ken Robinson decided he felt no hatred for the

Germans, but still didn't see the men of *Bismarck* as victims of an injustice.

> '*I wouldn't have liked to be on that ship, but I don't think you could call it revenge. We thought justice had been done, mainly, and we were out to get it mind you. In fact, everybody was determined to avenge the Hood, but it is the wrong word, really, to me. In the Navy, mainly we didn't have to kill civilians, women and children and whatnot. There really was no personal animosity because I think the Germans respected our way of fighting and we respected theirs. Regardless of what went on with the Jews — that was never going to be excused — the Navy was different.*'

Having seen the panorama of death and destruction laid out below their Swordfish aircraft, Terry Goddard and his fellow flyers felt that, while it was a necessary killing, it left a bad taste.

> '*Of course there was recognition Bismarck had to be sunk, but there was a deep feeling that it had been carried too far, that, for whatever reason, it had been too much. Of course Bismarck's motives were wrong — that's not hard to see — and everybody recognises that*

> *Hood's officers and men deserved a better fate.*
> *But our general feeling was: "Is it wrong to also*
> *think the Bismarck's officers and men deserved*
> *a better fate than being left in the water?".'*

Aboard the *Rodney*, shrugging off a lacklustre attack
by Luftwaffe bombers on her way back to the Clyde,
there was a keen awareness in Len Nicholl that while
the *Bismarck* may have gone, the German battleship
threat was not yet finished.

> *'Coming away after we had sunk Bismarck,*
> *we all took a deep sigh of relief to think at*
> *least we have got rid of one of them. When*
> *will it come about that we meet the Tirpitz?*
> *I thought that if the Tirpitz ever got out, she*
> *could cause as much damage as her sister ship*
> *did.'*

After her Boston refit, Admiral Tovey would for a
time ensure he had the heavy-hitting, proven battleship killer *Rodney* close at hand to meet *Tirpitz* if she
dared break out into the Atlantic.

For *Rodney's* Yves Dias, one of the youngest sailors
on the bridge of the ship throughout the final clash,
there was recognition that he had done well in his
baptism of fire. Rigid social barriers that prevented
commissioned officers and even senior ratings from

mixing off-duty aboard ship were temporarily washed away by the elation of surviving the battle. After recovering from the effects of a few post-battle tots of rum with the senior ratings down in their mess, his sober analysis was as follows:

> 'The whole point was that the Bismarck had to be sunk, no matter what. It was still heart-rending really to leave all these sailors in the icy sea who were obviously going to die, to just drown.'

With Colours Flying

In later composing his official report on the *Bismarck* Action, Home Fleet commander Admiral Tovey paid tribute to the heroism of the enemy.

> The BISMARCK had put up a most gallant fight against impossible odds, worthy of the old days of the Imperial German Navy, and she went down with her colours still flying.

It was his verdict that the *Bismarck* was, after around 90 minutes of pounding, 'in a sinking condition, and the final torpedoes from *Dorsetshire* only hastened her end'.

In his official report, Tovey also noted that there had been some casualties in the cruiser *Sheffield* and vessels of the 4th Destroyer Flotilla – caused by shell splinters from *Bismarck* near misses, with three men killed in *Sheffield* – but 'no casualties or damage to any of our ships during the subsequent day action'.

But, if the *Rodney's* splinter damage and injured rating were taken into account, this wasn't strictly true. Overall, however, the destruction of the *Bismarck* was as one-sided as the battle in which the *Hood* was blown apart.

Yet there have been claims and counter claims down the years about who, or what, exactly sank the *Bismarck*.

Gerhard Junack maintained after the war that, as he watched the *Bismarck* turn turtle and sink, there were no signs of torpedo damage, but wreck surveys since the conflict have found that is not true.

Aside from the *Bismarck's* superstructure and main turrets being torn apart, there were hundreds of holes in her due to the British bombardment, and she was rapidly flooding by the end. During the final battle, *Norfolk* fired 528 x 8-inch shells, *Dorsetshire* 254 x 8-inch, while *Rodney* fired 380 x 16-inch and 716 x 6-inch shells, and *King George V* 339 x 14-inch and 660 x 5.25-inch shells.

Between 300 and 400 shells hit the *Bismarck*, and yet the German battleship scored not a single hit on any of her assailants on 27 May.

The renowned wreck explorer David Mearns conducted a detailed examination of the wreck in the early 2000s. He concluded that, never mind the shell holes in her hull, between six and nine torpedoes punched holes in the *Bismarck* below the waterline – up to three dropped by Swordfish and as many as six launched by warships – a dreadful punishment compounded by the ship's own scuttling charges. Mearns has suggested that, even without the scuttling charges, the *Bismarck* would have sunk within minutes, hastened by the *Dorsetshire*'s multiple torpedo *coup de grace*.

It doesn't matter what or who exactly caused the battleship's sinking. The *Bismarck* was cornered by the British and destroyed as a fighting unit even before she disappeared below the waves.

War at sea is not a game of top trumps, nor can the reality of the *Bismarck*'s horrific end be obscured by technicalities.

With the guns falling silent, two of the British vessels that came to avenge the horrifying deaths of 1,415 men and boys on the *Hood* tried to save some of the *Bismarck*'s crew. That, above all, gave hope for humanity to prevail amid the horrors of war.

Beyond the terrible loss of ships and human life, the result of the *Bismarck* Action proved once again that British sea power could not be overcome by German battleships.

During the First World War, the Germans had constructed an entire fleet of battleships to take on an even bigger British navy. Despite this, in the famous words of an American newspaper commentary after the Battle of Jutland in May 1916, 'the German navy is still a navy in gaol which assaults its gaoler now and then but remains in gaol nevertheless.'

In May 1941, the allegedly most modern, powerful battleship in the world had proved – after a fighting life lasting just four days – that nothing had changed.

The Kriegsmarine was too small, lacking the flexible critical mass and mastery of the sea to beat the Royal Navy. The Kriegsmarine's battleship victory of late May 1941 ended its surface raiding against convoys. The *Bismarck*'s sister ship, *Tirpitz*, would spend most of the war hiding in the Norwegian fjords.

After numerous attempts by Royal Navy midget submarines and both Fleet Air Arm and RAF aircraft, she was sunk on 13 November 1944, off Hakøy Island, just across the water from Tromso. RAF Lancaster heavy bombers used so-called 'earthquake bombs' and, like the *Bismarck*, she capsized, taking 1,000 of her 2,400 men with her. Ultimately, as also happened in the First World War, Germany would turn to U-boats in order to deliver the victory battleships could not – by destroying Britain's convoy system. That strategy, too, would also end in failure.

The *Bismarck* Action helped convince world opinion the anti-fascist cause was viable and was particularly persuasive in the USA. The full might of the 'arsenal of democracy' (as President Franklin Roosevelt so memorably described it) would ultimately be unleashed against Germany. The flow of supplies and eventually armies, air forces and fleets from the USA to fight the Nazis could not be stopped. On the evening of 27 May 1941, President Roosevelt made a radio address to the American nation from the White House – his latest so-called 'Fireside Chat' – in which he declared 'an unlimited national emergency'. According to the *New York Times*, this was a move taken only when the USA's political leadership believed war was imminent.

The President slammed the Nazis and their plans 'for world domination' and made it clear the USA would not permit the Germans to win the Battle of the Atlantic, which extended 'from the icy waters of the North Pole to the frozen continent of the Antarctic.' He added:

> *'Throughout this huge area, there have been sinkings of merchant ships in alarming and increasing numbers by Nazi raider or submarines.'*

Roosevelt told his nation that the USA would help the British, by building vessels to replace the merchant ships they had lost and also via the US Navy (USN) 'helping to cut down the losses on the high seas'. The President told Americans:

> 'I say that the delivery of needed supplies to Britain is imperative. I say that this can be done; it must be done; and it will be done.'

Within months, the USN was involved in an undeclared war against the U-boats in the North Atlantic, bloodied even before it officially joined hostilities at year's end.

Calling out the fascist supporters in his own midst who suggested America should not help Britain, on the night of the *Bismarck*'s sinking, Roosevelt also explained:

> 'We will not accept a Hitler-dominated world. And we will not accept a world, like the post-war world of the 1920s, in which the seeds of Hitlerism can again be planted and allowed to grow.'

In August 1941, HMS *Prince of Wales* took a delegation led by Winston Churchill to Placentia Bay, Newfoundland, where – aboard that battleship and a US Navy cruiser – he and Roosevelt laid down a plan to fight for democracy against the totalitarians.

On 7 December 1941, Japan attacked the US Navy base at Pearl Harbor and devastated the Pacific Fleet by sinking most of its battleships. Hitler declared war on America four days later.

Japan also launched a campaign of conquest across Asia that aimed to topple European colonial powers and kick the Americans out of the Philippines, supplanting them all with its own 'Co-prosperity sphere'.

The scythe of what was now a truly global war at sea would also cut down British ships, some of whom had been the victors of the *Bismarck* Action.

The Wheel Turns

HMS *Prince of Wales* & HMS *Repulse*

The battleship HMS *Prince of Wales*, which had duelled with the *Bismarck* and landed blows that were pivotal to deciding the outcome of the May 1941 episode, was herself sunk on 10 December the same year.

After carrying Churchill to his August meeting with Roosevelt in Newfoundland and seeing action on the Malta convoy run that September, the *Prince of Wales* was sent on a forlorn mission to Singapore with the battlecruiser *Repulse*. Their aim was to try and deter the Japanese from invading by their mere presence in those waters.

Three days after Imperial Japanese Navy (IJN) aircraft carriers launched their strikes on USN's battle fleet at Pearl Harbor, IJN land-based aircraft were directed onto target by scouting reports from submarines that had trailed the British vessels. The *Prince of Wales* and *Repulse* were sunk off Malaya with a combined loss of 840 RN sailors and Royal Marines.

Just as the *Ark Royal*'s Swordfish had done for *Bismarck*, so Japanese torpedo-bombers crippled the *Prince of Wales*, shattering her steering and leaving her helpless to avoid destruction. It was the first time in history that aircraft had managed to sink enemy capital ships during a battle without assistance from the guns of surface warships.

One of the survivors was junior rating Joseph Willetts who, during the battle with *Bismarck* and *Prinz Eugen* in the Denmark Strait, had helped feed cordite charges to the guns of *Prince of Wales*.

Six months later, safely aboard the destroyer *Express* after abandoning ship, Willetts watched the *Prince of Wales* turn turtle and begin to slide under. Standing beside him was a Petty Officer who told Willetts:

> *'I'm going back… I'm not going to leave the lads there.'*

The Petty Officer dove into the sea and swam back to *Prince of Wales* never to be seen again.

HMS *Electra*

The destroyer that saved the *Hood*'s trio of survivors was likewise sunk in combat with the Japanese –

a fate her men surely suspected might come their way after the events of December 1941. *Electra* had helped to escort *Prince of Wales* and *Repulse* when they were attacked, her sailors watching helplessly as enemy torpedoes and bombs sank the capital ships.

Afterwards, the *Electra* rescued survivors from *Repulse*. The destroyer's Lt Timothy Cain looked on in horror as, in the distance, a whirlpool created by the *Prince of Wales* sinking wiped away hundreds of men fighting for their lives in the sea 'like chalk figures from a slate'.

In late February 1942, during the Battle of the Java Sea, the *Electra* charged through smoke in a running battle with more powerful enemy warships and was brought to a juddering halt by multiple shell hits.

Ninety-five of *Electra*'s 145-strong ship's company were killed.

U-74

German vessels caught up in the *Bismarck* Action were also among those soon claimed. *U-74*, which had rescued three of the *Bismarck*'s men, and throughout her career sank four merchant ships, one warship, and damaged three other enemy vessels, was herself destroyed off Spain, less than a year after the *Bismarck* Action. Her persecutors were relentless

British destroyers. All 47 of the U-boat's men were lost.

U-556

U-556 survived only until 27 June 1941, when she was cornered to the south of Iceland by three British corvettes protecting the UK-bound convoy HX-133. Running in on the surface for her torpedo attack, *U-556* used mist as a cover. Kapitänleutnant Wohlfahrt was forced to order a crash dive when it suddenly cleared. A circling Sunderland flying boat spotted the German submarine close to the surface and called in the escort vessels.

After five hours under assault and 54 depth charge explosions, the shambolic state of *U-556* – with numerous leaks and wrecked machinery – persuaded Wohlfahrt that annihilation was imminent without decisive action.

Two submariners, with their nerves shredded by the pummelling of their boat, had already pleaded with him to surface, but Wohlfahrt had threatened to shoot them if they did not return to their action stations.

Unlike the previous month, when he had raged at his own impotence, this time Wohlfahrt had the weapons to hit back. Taking a periscope look, he decided to put a torpedo into at least one of his persecutors before surfacing and, hopefully, escaping on the surface at high speed.

U-556 broke the surface in a barely controlled fashion, the enemy warships charging, and hurling depth charges set to explode almost instantly. They opened fire on the U-boat using their 4-inch main guns, with one shell ripping through the submarine's conning tower.

With the Engima machine, its rotors, and code-books already destroyed, Wolhfahrt ordered his men to abandon ship and the boat was scuttled. All but five of *U-556*'s 46-strong crew survived, while her captain spent the rest of the war in a prison camp, returning to Germany in 1947.

KM *Sachsenwald* & KM *Prinz Eugen*

The *Sachsenwald*, which had picked up two of the *Bismarck*'s men, was not sunk until August 1944. She was claimed by Allied naval forces when the latter ravaged a convoy the former trawler was escorting in the Bay of Biscay.

The *Prinz Eugen*, which also fought the *Hood* and the *Prince of Wales* in the Denmark Strait, found her bid to attack Allied convoys after parting company with *Bismarck* came to nothing.

Having headed towards the Azores, after taking on fuel from a tanker – and then meeting two other

German auxiliary supply vessels (to ask if they had seen any likely prey) – the heavy cruiser was afflicted by engine trouble.

Heading for Brest and joining forces with the *Scharnhorst* and *Gneisenau*, the *Prinz Eugen* made it back to Germany in February 1942, during the Channel Dash, when the British failed utterly to stop the enemy vessels slipping through the Channel.

But later the same month, during a foray into Norwegian waters, the *Prinz Eugen* was torpedoed by a British submarine, her stern breaking away. A number of sailors and soldiers aboard were killed.

The ill-starred *Prinz Eugen* was relegated to training duties, but in late 1944, when called on to provide naval gunfire support for troops trying to hold back the Red Army as it rolled towards the Baltic coast, she collided with the light cruiser *Leipzig*.

Surrendered to the Allies in May 1945; the *Prinz Eugen* was given to the Americans. They eventually parked her at Bikini Atoll, alongside other redundant vessels to study the effects of an atom bomb detonation during nuclear testing.

4th Destroyer Flotilla & ORP *Piorun*

When it comes to Vian's intrepid 4th Destroyer Flotilla that attacked the *Bismarck* on the night of 26 May, there were casualties there too, with the *Sikh* and *Zulu* lost in the Mediterranean during September 1942.

The *Piorun* was, however, a lucky ship and came through unharmed despite further action as an escort on the Malta convoy runs, the Atlantic convoys, during anti-shipping raids off Norway, and helping to cover Allied invasions of Italy and Normandy. She was handed back to the Royal Navy in 1946 and, after almost a decade in reserve, was sent to be broken up.

HMS *Maori*

The *Maori* only lasted until February 1942 but packed in more action between rescuing the *Bismarck*'s men and meeting her own end. In December 1941, during the Battle of Cape Bon, the *Maori* went into action alongside the *Sikh*, *Legion*, and Dutch destroyer *Isaac Sweers*.

British codebreakers had gained insight into an Italian plan to run supplies to Tripoli, and so the destroyers were sent to ambush the cruisers *Alberico da Barbiano* and *Alberto di Giussano* off Tunisia – both carrying cased oil. 'I think it took three or four minutes ... to sink both the Italian cruisers,' recalled Lieutenant Innes Hamilton.

'I should add that we were in a position to see the Italian ships but because we were on

the shore side [at night]. They could not see us against the Cape Bon Peninsula, and so it was very bad luck, if I can put it like that, on the Italians. [Aboard Maori] the alarm rattlers went, indicating that something was amiss. It just happened that we had [aboard] a colonel of the Argyll and Sutherlands who was taking passage from Gibraltar to Malta and we had a glass of port [on] the table [in the wardroom].

I said to the colonel: "We better go up onto the bridge quickly."

By the time we got there the two Italian cruisers were in flames … and we steamed past these flaming wrecks. It was with difficulty that we managed to avoid them and not actually run into them. It was the most incredible action. It took literally a matter of a few minutes. The two cruisers were sinking and that was it. There was no question of stopping to pick up the Italian sailors as they could virtually swim to Cape Bon or be rescued from there. We arrived in Malta and I have never seen anything like the welcome … the cheer as we came into harbour was terrific.'

The *Maori* was thereafter occupied with escorting convoys from Alexandria to Malta at a time when the British naval bastion was 'practically at its last gasp', according to Hamilton. The heroic actions of the merchant vessels and their naval escorts kept the island resupplied.

With Malta under intense bombardment from the air, courtesy of the Luftwaffe and Italian air force, on the night of 12 February 1942, a lone enemy aircraft was lost over the island and while seeking to head home, decided to unburden itself of bombs.

One of them hit the *Maori* 'and blew the ship virtually in half' according to Innes Hamilton 'partly because the torpedo warheads were detonated'…

> *'We were all asleep at the time; It was dark. It was all totally unexpected. The ship caught fire partly because the oil fuel tanks were ruptured and the sea in the harbour was covered in burning oil fuel.'*

Fortunately, most of the crew were in accommodation ashore, but nine of the ship's company lost their lives, either killed on the night or dying later of their wounds. It was Hamilton's job as First Lieutenant to look after the sailors who were aboard ship and try to save the *Maori* if he could.

> *'The engineer officer and I swam 'round the burning oil from the after end of the ship and*

got back onboard at the forward end. We did our best to keep the ship afloat. We started at the foremost end – the bow end – and cleared each compartment and closed all the doors and hammered them home, until we came to those parts of the ship which were so ruptured that they could not be made watertight. We then abandoned ship.

'*The rest of the ship's company without loss, all swam to the [nearby cruiser] Penelope. That was quite an achievement considering the burning oil on the sea.*

'*I am proud to say that the ship remained afloat for 36 hours but finally the weight of water burst the compartments and she finally sank. It was the end of a ship which had a brilliant life and had the most marvellous ship's company of West Country sailors who are unequalled in the world.*

'*I arrived alongside the Penelope in my pyjama trousers and that was all.*'

Innes Hamilton ended up serving in the *Penelope* and, by 1943, was captain of the destroyer HMS *Montgomery* and Escort Group W6 during the Battle of the Atlantic. He then commanded the frigate HMS *Dacres* for the Normandy landings of summer

1944 but had to give up that command due to damaged eyesight and hearing likely suffered during the bombing of *Maori*.

After an unsuccessful bid as a Liberal Party candidate in the General Election of 1945, Hamilton was appointed as a staff officer in British Pacific Fleet (BPF) on Victory over Japan Day (15 August 1945). He got as far as Sydney, Australia before his new job was cancelled.

When it came to pondering the ships that brought him through the war, it was the *Maori* that earned first place in his heart.

> *'I joined the ship before she was completed … and left her last when she was sunk, so I have a tremendous affection for the ship [which] I served in her throughout her career.'*

HMS *Cossack*

The *Cossack* met her nemesis on 23 October 1941, to the west of Portugal as she escorted a UK-bound convoy. *U-563* hit the *Cossack* with one torpedo that blew off the front of the ship, killing 159 of her crew. There were 60 survivors.

Ken Robinson was not there. He had broken his arm when the ship was alongside in Scotland, slipping on the destroyer's upper deck while carrying a box of ammunition. Taken to a hospital in Glasgow, he was there for three months. 'I read about *Cossack*'s end in the paper,' he recalled, 'and it was like a severe blow'…

> 'A shock it was, really – "How can they sink my ship?" A torpedo from a submarine had hit a for'ard ammunition magazine. It blew a lot of the ship away, killed nearly everybody on the bridge and everyone forward, more or less, of the break in the foc'sle. After a while they abandoned ship. Some were picked up by HMS Carnation, some by HMS Legion. The Carnation then put some back onboard and they got the pumps working and started to pump out water and I think it was the Carnation took it in tow. Cossack was towed for two days, trying to get back. Eventually it was that bad they just had to let it go.'

There but for the grace of God went Robinson who was instead left to mourn lost shipmates.

> 'It was the big loss of life that was the shock. There was one or two that you knew but inevitably – even in a small ship like a destroyer – there were a lot of them you wouldn't know. You wouldn't get to know stokers, for example.

They had their own messes and worked in a different part of the ship that we seamen never went. Stokers went ashore together; seamen went ashore together. Yet you always chatted to them because it was a very friendly ship. It was my own mess mates that I thought about mainly.'

HMS *Ark Royal* / Swordfish

Another of the *Bismarck* Action participants that fell victim to a U-boat torpedo was *Ark Royal*. While Terry Goddard had already left the ship, he was there to witness her slow demise. A month before she was torpedoed, he had been transferred to an older, smaller carrier, the First World War vintage HMS *Argus*, in command of two Swordfish. On 13 November 1941, the *Ark* and *Argus* were returning to Gibraltar after a mission to ferry fighter planes to Malta and were sighted by *U-81*. The torpedo hit created a large hole, but the *Ark* did not immediately sink. Remarkably, only one of *Ark*'s crew was killed. But aircraft in the task group, including Goddard's, were scrambled.

'I couldn't get off quick enough with a submarine around, so I flew off the Argus and carried out an anti-submarine patrol around

the ships as they went scuttling back to harbour. I stayed around the Ark until just before dusk. Argus had long gone, so we went back and landed at North Front airfield in Gibraltar. I guess we were the first to announce to the people there that Ark had been torpedoed, which was not very nice.'

Even though she was towed almost to safety, the *Ark* finally succumbed around 30 miles from safe harbour, and Goddard thought it 'a pitiful ending'.

'We were fiddling around doing exercises outside Gib. Had we gone straight in to port, Ark would probably still be alive. I know it is conjecture on my part, but the general feeling was that, had damage control been properly carried out, Ark would have been able to get back to harbour.'

By April 1942, Goddard was CO of 803 Squadron, a Fulmar fighter-reconnaissance unit, embarked in HMS *Formidable*, deployed to the Far East.

'And then the Japanese raided the Indian Ocean. We high tailed it down to some atoll or other. All we heard was reports coming in from ships all over the place that they were being

sunk. Five of the Formidable's six Fulmars were lost, which left us very much depleted. We were carrying out single plane combat air patrols, during one of which we intercepted a Jap aircraft. We got involved in a dogfight. At the end, he came roaring up our stern. I opened fire with the Bren gun. He was no further than about 30 yards away. I know I hit him, but we didn't claim that he was shot down because, just at that moment, we went into a high-speed stall, which went on forever. I open up the hood. I am watching the altimeter. I am getting ready to bail out when we finally pull out of the stall. I guess we are at a thousand feet, maybe lower. Nelson, the pilot, is so shattered we don't go back to fight. We just scurry back to Formidable. Then of course we heard that Cornwall and Dorsetshire had been sunk...'

HMS *Dorsetshire* & HMS *Cornwall*

Less than a year after delivering the final blows to *Bismarck*, the *Dorsetshire* herself was claimed. She and sister heavy cruiser *Cornwall* were sunk by Japanese aircraft in the Indian Ocean on the same day.

By then, the *Dorsetshire* had a new Commanding Officer, Captain Gus Agar, who won the Victoria

Cross just after the First World War, for a daring attack on Soviet warships in the Baltic.

Many of the *Dorsetshire* sailors who saw *Bismarck* sunk, and helped rescue some of her men, were killed by the Japanese air attack on that fateful day in spring 1942. The *Dorsetshire* had just escorted a troopship full of women and children to safety in Australia and also evacuated people from Singapore. She was then ordered to Colombo in Ceylon to get new anti-aircraft guns fitted and receive other work.

On 4 April, the *Dorsetshire* was ordered to immediately join the Eastern Fleet in the Indian Ocean, which was at the time 400-500 miles away.

Some people did not make it back before the ship sailed in company with *Cornwall*. They were the lucky ones. While still around 300 miles from the fleet, the two cruisers were pounced on by Japanese carrier aircraft.

George Bell was at a new action station, as the communication rating in A turret of the 8-inch guns.

> 'They came out of the sun, right down and attacked us. We thought if they were torpedo-carrying planes, we could lower the 8-inch guns and fire at them like *Bismarck* did at our planes with her 15-inch.'

Unfortunately, the enemy dive-bombers were impossible to hit with the 8-inch guns while the new AA weapons were only tied to *Dorsetshire's* upper deck and so not properly mounted. They could not be trained or fired, leaving the cruiser with minimal defence against air attack. She suffered 23 hits aft of the bridge that took out the engine room and steering, killing and wounding hundreds of men. Bell received the order to abandon ship.

> *'I passed the message to the officer in charge of the turret, and he passed it out to the gun's crew. I remember vividly, even now, taking my phone set off, switching it off and hanging it up in its proper place as if I'd be coming back. Our instructions always were put your lifebelt on and only partly blow it up, just enough to float but not to stop you from swimming. I climbed down out of the turret onto the deck. Because the ship was already listing over very badly, we had to climb up the deck to get to the ship's side… You had to make sure you left the ship on the opposite side to where she was going over or you'd be sucked underneath.*
>
> *'I slid down across the ship's hull, into the sea and swam away to get as far away before it turned over. I got probably couple of hundred*

yards away, with two or three other sailors.
Suddenly we heard guns. The Japanese were
coming down and machine-gunning us. There
is only one thing to do to avoid machine gun
bullets and that is to get under the water. We
dove under. I came back up and fortunately
was alright. The chap next to me had been
shot the whole length of his back with machine
gun bullets. He had his lifebelt blown up too
high and didn't go under the water.

'After that we all gathered together.'

The *Cornwall* had been sunk about a mile away. She
took 15 minutes to be overwhelmed and sink, while
the *Dorsetshire* lasted just ten. *Dorsetshire's* wounded
were put into two lifeboats that had somehow avoided
being holed during the Japanese assault. The rest of
the 500 survivors, including Bell, sat on rafts, perched
on wreckage, or clung onto pieces of wood. The
water was at least warm, and the few sharks swimming
around luckily didn't come anywhere near Bell.

'It was said they don't like dead bodies. There
was also a lot of oil fuel about and there was
people splashing around in the water. That was
late afternoon and it soon became dark. Going
through your mind was the question of whether

*or not we would be picked up, but we thought
our own fleet would know where we were.'*

A British scout aircraft had spotted them but was shot
down by the Japanese before it could pass the message
on.

*'I felt I could last it out, as I was physically
fit, wasn't injured in any way. After dark you
kept seeing the odd light and thinking it was a
ship, but it was the stars coming up. Daybreak
came and there was still no ship.*

*'We just said: "Well, we hope something
will turn up, so long as it's not the Japanese."'*

Bell was sitting on a wooden trestle just big enough to
keep him afloat. Nearby there was a Carley float with
wounded aboard. Overnight, Bell heard a splash as
someone tumbled off a raft, having fallen asleep and
losing their balance. There was much swearing and
shouting as the raft itself lost balance and everybody
else was tipped off, too.

*'During the course of the second day, we had
half a biscuit each and a little sip of water. Of
course it got pretty warm later on and, as time
wore on, we thought:*

*"'Well that's it, we have got past the 24
hours' time in the water during which we can*

reasonably expect rescue." We began to wonder how we would survive another night. This was all going through your mind.

'Late afternoon, a plane was sighted indicating that help was on its way. Just as it was getting dark these two destroyers and a cruiser came up – the Paladin, Panther, and Enterprise.

'It was just getting towards seven o'clock in the evening when the Paladin came around to us and started to actually pick us up, get the wounded onboard. They launched a boat because some of us were not capable of getting up the side of the ship. The rest of us swam towards the ship and there were scrambling nets over the side. We were pulled up onto the ship and they plied us with hot tea.

'All we wanted to do was find a quiet corner and curl up and go to sleep. I remember somebody giving me a blanket, which was greatly appreciated, as all I had been wearing when I abandoned ship was just a pair of shorts. Most of us were like that, as it was standard dress in the tropics inside a hot warship.

'Two or three hundred of us ended up in the Paladin. There seemed to be more survivors *than crew packed into what was only a small destroyer.'*

The three rescue ships set course for the Maldives, leaving behind 234 men in the *Dorsetshire* and 190 in *Cornwall* on the bottom of the ocean.

HMS *Rodney*

Yves Dias left the *Rodney* after the *Bismarck* Action and saw further war service in three destroyers on convoy escort work, protecting the kind of ships he had sailed in as an apprentice Merchant Navy officer. He was navigator of HMS *Meteor* on convoys to Russia and also across the North Atlantic.

> *'We seemed to spend an awful lot of time on the bridge, closed up at action stations. I used to sleep on the bridge because it was a bit hazardous to go along a destroyer's deck in a gale, in anything other than a flat calm, in fact. It was chilly to say the least on an open bridge. I regularly felt concerned we might get torpedoed – it was a case of crossed-fingers and say a prayer.*
>
> *'I remember I saw oil tankers being hit and one or two ammunition ships. The latter just disappeared in a big bang. That was on*

a transatlantic convoy and most of the U-boat attacks happened at night. With oil tankers the thing was on fire and the sea was on fire. And so, to even get rescued, survivors would have to swim through burning oil. Terrible. In fact, one of the chaps burned to death in that sort of situation was the brother of a fellow apprentice on the San Alberto. He was on another ship in the same convoy and had to watch his brother die.

'My tanker hadn't caught fire in 1939 because it was empty – we were outward bound to collect a cargo but, had we been homeward bound, it might have been entirely different. I am just glad that we won the war and proud to have been in it, but sad beyond all thought that it killed so many, that it cost so many men...'

Len Nicholl also left the *Rodney* to see war further service, in his case a carrier fighting the Japanese. He manned an anti-aircraft gun mounted in a rather exposed position on the rim of the flight deck of *Victorious*, another veteran vessel from the *Bismarck* Action. This time the carrier was not sending Sword-fish to attack an enemy battleship but launching air raids by US-supplied monoplane fighter-bombers. On 9 May 1945, off the island of Okinawa, the

Victorious and rest of the British Pacific Fleet were subjected to a determined assault by kamikaze aircraft.

> 'One hit the ship for'ard and killed eight of the lads on A turret on the port side and their officer later died of his wounds. The other lad that got killed that same day was on his own in a gun position. The Kamikaze plane just skidded across the deck, as its bomb didn't explode. It slid off over the side. Some of the lads on my gun deck fired their Oerlikons at the wreckage as it was going past. I saw the Formidable hit with two suiciders, and the smoke and flames that came up from that was terrific.
>
> 'You'd have thought she would have been out of action for the rest of the war, but she wasn't. Formidable was back in action a couple of days afterwards, as were we. I think we got hit by these suiciders on the day they celebrated the end of the war in Europe, VE Day … and you can imagine our feelings out there, completely ignored really.
>
> 'The thing is the kamikazes were so fanatical. They didn't believe in capitulating, did they? When they dropped the atom bombs, we were only too pleased to think that the war

had ended. I couldn't believe it, once we went into Japan afterwards. They were a completely different people. It seemed such a peaceful country as opposed to what we expected from fighting them.'

HMS *Rodney* didn't ever see action against the Japanese, for she was too old and worn out to take such a long voyage to face them. Seeing off attacks by Stuka dive-bombers and submarines during the Operation Pedestal convoy run to Malta in August 1942, further service saw the battleship supporting the Allied invasion of North Africa and then using her 16-inch guns to pound German troops in Normandy during the summer of 1944.

Cranky though she was – with some parts of her hull cemented in place and the propulsion increasingly temperamental – *Rodney* was required to accompany an Allied convoy to northern Russia in autumn 1944, just in case the *Tirpitz* came out of her Norwegian fjord lair.

Tirpitz decided on that occasion not to emerge, but the *Rodney* was held in the Orkneys as the Home Fleet flagship just in case. She was sent out for gunnery practice regularly to prepare for a fight with the *Bismarck*'s battle-shy sister ship.

On 27 November, reconnaissance photographs taken by an RAF aircraft arrived aboard *Rodney*.

The battleship's officers studied them keenly, for they revealed the *Tirpitz* was finally finished, having turned turtle after being hit by up to three 12,000lbs bombs dropped by RAF Lancaster bombers.

The *Rodney* could at last stand down and in early 1946 was decommissioned, being finally sent for scrap in the spring of 1948.

A Timeless Lesson

The knowledge that the cruel wheel of fate brings death and disaster in war as surely as it brings glory is a timeless lesson of the *Bismarck* Action. Such is the peculiar nature of things.

People who you once tried to kill – and who were also trying to kill you – even turned out to be the kind of folk you could relate to and admire.

With the end of hostilities, and the passing of time, the survivors of the *Bismarck* formed a bond with the men of the *Maori* and *Dorsetshire* who had rescued them in May 1941. At joint reunions in Britain and Germany, they toasted absent comrades.

And among those attending was Otto Peters, who, for all the trauma and tragedy he experienced, regarded the *Bismarck* as 'a special ship ... a proud ship' while also holding the men who sank her in high esteem. The Britons and Germans were united by their experiences of war.

'The British sailors had the same feeling that we had. They were great. I must say that. We met after the war almost every year.'

Postscript

'...any man's death diminishes me,
because I am involved in mankind.
And therefore never send to know for whom
the bell tolls; it tolls for thee.'

—John Donne, 'XVII. Meditation.'

Usually engraved with a ship's name and commissioning date, a ship's bell tolls to denote the time, which is especially important for watch-keepers at sea.

Through the centuries, ship's bells have also been used to sound the alarm and even to christen babies in. A ship's bell therefore holds a special place in the heart of sailors.

Like the crews of other ships, the sailors and Royal Marines of the HMS *Hood* considered their bell to be a reassuring part of their daily lives, even a talisman. When shipwreck hunter David Mearns explored the remains of the *Hood* in the early 2000s, he found the ship's bell but dared not even touch it, never mind use a remotely operated vehicle (ROV) to recover it.

This was out of respect for the war grave status of the wreck.

It was when the *Hood* survivor Ted Briggs, and others with connections to the ship, told him that recovering the bell would be a wonderful thing that Mearns started pondering the feasibility of a return expedition to do just that.

In August 2012, having earlier gained permission from the UK defence ministry to proceed, this duly happened. It was enabled by the support of Microsoft co-founder Paul G Allen who provided his cutting-edge ocean exploration ship the *Octopus* as the base for the recovery bid. Due to stormy weather it failed, but a second attempt in 2015 was successful.

Ted Briggs had passed away in 2008, but Rear Admiral Philip Wilcocks was able to assist Mearns during his attempts to recover the bell.

Wilcocks had been captain of the destroyer HMS *Gloucester* in the 1991 Gulf War, and was, at one time, boss of the Royal Navy frigate and destroyer force. But he also had a special connection to the *Hood*. His uncle went down with the ship.

Nineteen-year-old Able Seaman Eric Wilcocks was the youngest of three brothers who served in the

Royal Navy. During the Battle of the Denmark Strait, he was a gunner operating one of the 4-inch anti-aircraft guns on the *Hood*'s shelter deck. It is believed Eric was killed or wounded when an 8-inch shell from the *Prinz Eugen* hit that part of the ship.

When the 75th anniversary of the *Hood*'s loss was commemorated at Portsmouth naval dockyard in 2016, the Princess Royal struck eight bells at midday on the battlecruiser's bell.

Rear Admiral Wilcocks was there in his capacity as President of The *Hood* Association and explained the huge significance of the moment. 'There is no headstone among the flowers for those who perish at sea,' he said.

> *'For the 1,415 officers and men who lost their lives in HMS Hood on 24 May 1941, the recovery of her bell, and its subsequent place of honour in The National Museum of the Royal Navy in Portsmouth, will mean that future generations will be able to gaze upon her bell and remember with gratitude and thanks the heroism, courage, and personal sacrifice of Hood's ship's company who died in the service of their country.'*

Acknowledgements

In my head are two movie quotes, neither of which are made in the context of naval warfare but have somehow lodged as relevant to this story. In the telling, it is cinematic anyway, or aspires to be at least as cleanly structured as any movie, with a distinct beginning, middle, and end.

Bismarck destroys *Hood* and then escapes vengeance for a short while before being found again. She is hunted down and killed.

The End. Or is it?

In pondering that, I am reminded of something Gene Hackman's character in the movie *A Bridge Too Far* says and also of Laurence Olivier's portrayal of a senior air force officer in *The Battle of Britain*, both of which I saw at the cinema as a lad in the 1970s.

In the latter, Air Chief Marshal Hugh Dowding (Olivier) is in his office dealing with a bullish, over-confident government minister. The politician is dismayed by the RAF officer's rather downbeat assess-ment of the situation, especially his refusal to put all his faith in the new, supposedly war-winning, technology of radar. 'God willing, we will hold out, minister,' says a matter-of-fact Dowding, who later adds that he is 'trusting in God and praying for radar, but the essential arithmetic is that our young men will have to shoot down their young men at the rate of four to one, if we are to keep pace at all.'

In other words, old men talk (or write) about war, but it is the young men of each side that conduct its grim business by killing each other. The side that wins will most often, though not always, be the one that kills more than the other.

In *A Bridge Too Far* – about the disastrous bid by Allied airborne forces to leap across the Rhine into Germany in 1944 – Gene Hackman plays the Polish parachute brigade commander Stanislaw Sosabowski.

After the operation has failed, Sosabowski is involved in a discussion with some British and American senior officers about what caused it to become a disaster.

He tells them:

> *'It doesn't matter what it was. When one man says to another: "I know what, let's do today, let's play the war game"… everybody dies.'*

He means there are no winners in the end among the combatants, as I think this story also shows, to a certain extent, except perhaps those who survive to reach old age.

The aforementioned movie characters are fictional interpretations of real men in war, but what you have read here are the thoughts of real men in a real war.

I think only those who have been there can quite understand the full scope and brutal reality of it – and the mix of conflicting motivations aroused by the business of killing or being killed in combat.

–

Nothing is actually as clean as the average Hollywood plot. Hopefully, this account helps dispel some of the illusions some people may have about the *Bismarck* Action. Web forum arguments about gun calibres and armour thickness, who torpedoed what and when, along with claims that the British didn't *really* sink *Bismarck* are beside the point.

It is fitting we should hear directly from those who survived, thanks in no small measure to the filmed interviews I conducted with several veterans. It helps sort the myth from the reality (or irrelevant from relevant).

I am a long-time admirer of Nicholas Monsarrat's searing, unyielding fictional account of naval warfare in the Second World War, *The Cruel Sea*, which was based on his real-life experiences. For it was indeed a long, hard and, yes, cruel war at sea.

This book it is above all dedicated to those who risked their lives before, during, and after the *Bismarck* Action, and who allowed me to question them at length on camera, namely George Bell, Alfred Brimacombe, Yves Dias, Terry Goddard, Len Nicholl, and Ken Robinson.

It was a sometimes arduous process for men of advancing years. The transcripts of what they said – tweaked and polished very slightly here and there, to suit the different medium of a book, but otherwise as it came out of them – are what, hopefully, make this such an absorbing, immediate experience. They provide something truly special – a lasting memorial to what their generation did for us. Sadly, they have now crossed the bar.

I would also like to thank Stuart Antrobus, my friend and colleague, whom I first got to know in Arabia on the eve of the 1991 Gulf War. I later worked with him during several journalistic assignments, from the Balkans to the Baltic States, in Russia and elsewhere before embarking on this project in 2010. As a former member of the Naval Service himself, Stuart was enthusiastically committed to the cause of filming the veterans, despite a hectic schedule as a TV cameraman helping to send back the news from modern conflict zones.

In putting together this expanded and slightly revised edition of *Bismarck: 24 Hours to Doom* I have drawn on a slightly wider range of sources and some people have provided me with extra help. I would therefore like to extend my sincere thanks to: John Ruffer for giving me sight of his father Major JEM Ruffer's diary notes for the *Bismarck* Action (to supplement my 2009 contacts with Maj Ruffer while writing *Killing the Bismarck*); Rear Admiral Philip Wilcocks, president of the HMS *Hood* Association who shared some details of his uncle Eric with me; Paul Bevand, archivist of the *Hood* Association, for allowing me to draw on material posted on the very impressive web site run in honour of that famous warship; my good friend and fellow historian Capt Peter Hore, who gave me sight of relevant elements in his new book *Bletchley Park's Secret Source* and at various times discussed aspects of the *Bismarck* Action with me; Jamie Burnham for highlighting his grandfather's part in flying a reconnaissance mission over *Bismarck* on 26 May 1941; James Crawford for pointing me in the direction of a German TV documentary that featured his late father, Vice Admiral Sir William Crawford, which I viewed on YouTube. The latter supplemented other research, not least that carried out via the superb sound archive at the Imperial War Museum. I must not forget to once again convey my appreciation to Kevin Byers for providing the transcript of his late father Tommy talking about the final battle with *Bismarck*, and the original sound recording.

I also want to mention the late Rob McAuley – filmmaker and yachtsman – who kindly granted me permission to access transcripts of interviews with Allied and German veterans who were involved in the great battleship fights of the Second World War. For this book it has enabled me to use testimony from Peter Bridewell, Ted Briggs, Edmund Carver, Pat Jackson, Ludovic Kennedy, and Otto Peters.

I'd also like to express my thanks to Rear Admiral Martin Connell, at the time of publication head of the Fleet Air Arm, for writing the foreword. A former front-line naval aviator, he is today charged with overseeing the introduction into full operational service of the two new British aircraft carriers HMS *Queen Elizabeth* and HMS *Prince of Wales*.

Martin hosted me aboard the frigate HMS *Chatham* while in command of that warship during a 2008 patrol 'up threat' in the northern Arabian Gulf. In the same waters 17 years earlier, I met Philip Wilcocks on the bridge of the destroyer HMS

Gloucester, which he was then preparing for war as her captain.

Insights into the character and spirit of navies gained during numerous visits to warships on deployment around the world, including to *Chatham* and *Gloucester*, inform my writing about naval operations both past and present.

Renowned author of action-packed true-life thrillers about military and naval aviation history Rowland White and also best-selling seafaring novelist (and ex-RN officer) Julian Stockwin – author of the famous Thomas Kydd series – kindly agreed to endorse the book. That means a great deal to me, as I am a great admirer of their work.

Finally, at Agora Books, I must again express my gratitude to Sam Brace (who has edited this new edition) and Peyton Stableford both of whom have been immensely professional and enthusiastic. My thanks must also go to Canelo for creating the reprint editions of both *Arnhem* and *Bismarck*. I would like also to thank my agent Tim Bates and Kate Evans (2016 edition editor) at PFD for giving the green light to the original edition.

Sources

Museum/Archives

Imperial War Museum

Oral history interviews in the Sound Archive:

Crawford, William Godfrey – catalogue number 10673.

Hamilton, Kenneth Innes – catalogue number 15240.

Lang, John – catalogue number 12503.

Willetts, Joseph – catalogue number 8222.

Wisniewski, Pawel – catalogue number 30282.

US Naval History and Heritage Command

'The Sinking of the German Battleship *Bismarck* as Described in the FDU/BdU [Commander U-boats] War Log, 24-31 May 1941.'

The National Archives (UK)

ADM 234/509. Admiral Tovey's official despatch of the *Bismarck* Action.

ADM 186/806. C.B. 4051 (24). 'German Battleship *Bismarck* – Interrogation of Survivors.'

ADM 116/4351: 'Report on the Loss of HMS Hood.'

National Museum of the Royal Navy

'Conserved HMS Hood Bell Rings out on 75th Anniversary of Largest Ever Royal Navy Loss' – blog on NMRN web site www.nmrn.org.uk

Other

Collection of Major JEM Ruffer RMs

Contemporary diary notes taken by Major Ruffer, Royal Marines, 23–27 May 1941, while serving in the cruiser HMS *Norfolk*.

HMS Hood Association

'Remembering Hood – I was There, We Found Only Three' by Jack Taylor, sailor serving in HMS *Electra*.

'Biography of Robert E Tilburn' by Paul Bevand and Frank Allen (Approved by the Tilburn Family).'

All accessed via www.hmshood.com

Naval-History.Net

HMS *Maori* (F24) – Tribal Class Destroyer (service history).

Accessed via www.naval-history.net

KBismarck.com

'Fishing Vessel "Sachsenwald", Report regarding the Rescue Mission "Bismarck" 30 May 1941.' Translated from the German by Ulrich Rodofsky.

'The Last Hours of the *Bismarck*' by Gerhard Junack (originally published in 'Purnell's History of the Second World War', Vol 2, No 5,1967).

Accessed via www.KBismarck.com

U-boat Archive

CB 04051 (26). 'U-556 – Interrogation of Survivors.'

FDU/BdU [Commander U-boats] War Log, 16–31 May 1941.

Accessed via www.uboatarchive.net

Uboat.net

'U-74 and the Bismarck Tragedy' a blog by Gregor Lichtfuss.

Accessed via www.uboat.net

Paul Allen

'HMS Hood's Bell has Been Successfully Recovered' – blog in the web site www.paulallen.com

Legasee

'WWII – Keeping Britain Afloat', Legasee, online educational resource.

Accessed via www.legasee.org.uk

Liverpool Museums

'The Merchant Navy: Britain's Lifeline' (fact sheet), Merseyside Maritime Museum. www.liverpoolmuseums.org.uk

Miller Center, University of Virginia

'May 27, 1941: Fireside Chat 17: On an Unlimited National Emergency' – transcript of radio broadcast by President Franklin D Roosevelt.

Accessed via www.millercenter.org

Bomber Command Museum of Canada

'Sinking of the Battleship Tirpitz', blog on the web site.

Accessed via www.bombercommandmuseum.ca

World War II – Unit History & Officers, Royal Navy (RN) Officers 1939-1945

Tabulated bios of the following:

Hamilton, Kenneth, Innes.

Kennedy, Edward Coverley.

Kennedy, Ludovic Henry Coverley.

Accessed via www.unithistories.com

Interviews

Filmed in the UK and Canada 2010–2014

George Bell – Captain's messenger, HMS *Dorset-shire* (heavy cruiser).

Terry Goddard – Swordfish torpedo–bomber Observer, serving with squadron embarked in HMS *Ark Royal* (aircraft carrier).

Ken Robinson – Rating gunner, HMS *Cossack* (destroyer).

Yves Dias – Junior officer, HMS *Rodney* (battle-ship).

Len Nicholl – Royal Marine gunner, HMS *Rodney*.

Alfred Brimacombe – Stoker, HMS *Rodney*.

Captain Peter Hore – former Head of Defence Studies in the RN (expert analysis of the histor-ical context).

Interviewer. Iain Ballantyne.

Cameraman: Stuart Antrobus.

Also interviewed Terry Goddard (in Canada) using detailed list of questions supplied by Iain Ballantyne.

Audio Interview

Tommy Byers – Rating, HMS *Rodney* (supplied by his son Kevin Byers).

Interview Transcripts

Peter Bridewell – Rating gunner, HMS *King George V* (battleship).

Ted Briggs – Rating signaller, HMS *Hood* (battle-cruiser).

Edmund Carver – Swordfish pilot, squadron embarked in HMS *Ark Royal* (aircraft carrier).

Pat Jackson – Swordfish pilot, squadron embarked in HMS *Victorious* (aircraft carrier).

Ludovic Kennedy – Junior officer, HMS *Tartar* (destroyer).

Otto Peters – Engine room rating, KM *Bismarck* (battleship).

Material from all of the above used with kind permission of Rob McAuley. Original interviews for TV documentary series 'The Battleships' (a Rob McAuley Production for Channel 4, 2001).

Newspapers

The Advocate. Burnie, Tasmania, 30 May 1939, article entitled 'Great Britain's Immense Imports'.

Nelson Evening Mail. New Zealand, 7 June 1916.

The New York Times. 25 May and 28 May 1941.

Bibliography

A Bridge Too Far. Directed by Richard Attenborough, performances by Gene Hackman, Joseph E Levine Productions, 1977.

Ballantyne, Iain. *HMS Rodney.* Pen & Sword, 2008.

Ballantyne, Iain. *Killing the Bismarck*, Pen & Sword, 2014.

Ballantyne, Iain. *The Deadly Trade*, Weidenfeld & Nicolson, 2018.

Bercuson, J, and Herwig, Holger H. *Bismarck.* Hutchinson, 2002.

Blair, Clay. *Hitler's U-Boat War* – The Hunters 1939–1942. Cassell, 2000.

Brayley, Martin J. *The British Home Front* 1939–45. Osprey, 2012.

Brower, Jack. *The Battleship Bismarck.* Naval Institute Press, 2005.

Churchill, Winston. *The Second World War, Vol III*. Cassell, 1950.

Colville, John. *The Fringes of Power*. Phoenix, 2005.

Deighton, Len. *Blood, Tears and Folly*. Pimlico, 1995.

Dixon, Jeremy. *The U-Boat Commanders*. Pen & Sword, 2019.

Dönitz, Admiral Karl. *Memoirs*. Cassell, 2002.

Donne, John. 'XVII. Meditation.' *Devotions Upon Emergent Occasions*.

Draminski, Stefan. *The Battleship Scharnhorst*. Osprey 2021.

Edgerton, David. *Britain's War Machine*. Allen Lane, 2011.

Garzke, William H, Dulin, Robert O, Jurens, William. *Battleship Bismarck*. Naval Institute Press, 2019.

Grehan, John and Mace, Martin, compilers. *Capital Ships at War 1939-1945*. Pen & Sword, 2014.

Grenfell, Capt Russell. *The Bismarck Episode*. Faber and Faber, 1949.

Hore, Peter. *Bletchley Park's Secret Source*. Greenhill, 2021.

Kemp, Paul. *British Warship Losses of the 20th Century*. Sutton Publishing, 1999.

Kemp, Paul. *U-Boats Destroyed*. Weidenfeld & Nicolson, 1999.

Kennedy, Ludovic. *Pursuit*. Cassell, 2004.

Mearns, David, *The Shipwreck Hunter*. Allen & Unwin, 2017.

Monsarrat, Nicholas. *The Cruel Sea*. Penguin, 2002.

Von Müllenheim-Rechberg, Baron Burkard. *Battleship Bismarck*. Bodley Head, 1981.

Overy, Richard, ed. *The New York Times Complete World War II*. Black Dog & Leventhal, 2013.

Schofield, Vice Admiral BB. *Loss of the Bismarck*. Ian Allan, 1972.

Sink the Bismarck. Directed by Robert Kirk, ZDF, 1996. Broadcast 2003.

Showell, Jack Mailman, ed. *Fuehrer Conferences on Naval Affairs 1939-1945*. The History Press, 2015.

The Battle of Britain. Directed by Guy Hamilton, performances by Laurence Olivier, Spitfire Productions, 1969.

Wellings, Rear Admiral Joseph H. *On His Majesty's Service*. Naval War College Press, 1983.